Swordfish Special

W. A. Harrison

LONDON

IAN ALLAN LTD

First published 1977

ISBN 0 7110 0742 X

Published by Ian Allan Ltd, Shepperton, Surrey,
and printed in the United Kingdom by
Ian Allan Printing Ltd.

ACKNOWLEDGEMENTS

In any work of this kind where the author is not a full time
professional, a considerable amount of time must be spent outside
the normal family circle. I would, therefore, like to thank my wife
who was patient, understanding and there when I faltered. I can
never give the children back the lost time but hope that in future
years they will look at this work and believe that it was time well
spent. To the many individuals and organisations that helped me
I can only say — *Thank You*. Not in any sort of order they are;
Flight International; Hawker-Siddeley, Brough Division; Mr
Willis and Mr Lucas of the Department of Photographs, Imperial
War Museum; Mrs H. M. Hollister of the Research Department,
Fleet Air Arm Museum; Mr E. H. Turner of the RAF Air
Historical Branch; Paul Calderwood of The Fairey Co. Ltd;
Public Archives of Canada; Commander F. C. van Oosten,
Director of Naval History, Royal Netherlands Navy; National
Museum of Science and Technology, Canada; Fox Photos Ltd;
United States Navy; D. Becker of The Aviation Society of
Africa; J. T. Canham; B. J. Cooper; A. J. Jackson; P. Gifford; A.
H. Trigell; M. J. F. Bowyer; J. K. Cannon; N. Pocock; H. Levy;
Ian Huntley; Admiral Sir Frank Hopkins, KCB, DSO, DSC, RN,
(Retd); Rear Admiral J. A. Ievers, CB, OBE, RN, (Retd); Rear
Admiral P. D. Gick, CB, OBE, DSC, RN, (Retd); Captain L. E. D.
Walthall, DSC, RN, (Retd); Captain F. D. Howie, RN (Retd);
Commander J. H. Stenning, RN, (Retd); Commander R. N.
Everett, OBE, RN, (Retd); Commander S. H. Suthers, DSC, RN,
(Retd); Lt Cdr C. N. Wines, RN; Ltd Cdr G. M. T. Osborne, DSO,
DSC, RN, (Retd). and to the editor of *Punch* for permission to print
SWORDFISH by R.C.S.

Contents

Title page: A magnificent shot of K.8428 M on October 22, 1938 shortly after releasing its torpedo. The main difficulty was to put the torpedo into water at the right attitude so that it entered cleanly to begin its run. It was easy to get either speed or height wrong so that the torpedo plunged to the bottom or bounced off the surface and broke up. The fitting of a wooden 'airtail' made it possible to drop at higher altitudes and speeds later in the war. Based at Gosport with the TTU K.8428 had been delivered in February 1937 and was still flying with No.785 Training Squadron at Crail in November 1941./*Fox Photos*

Top left : LS.326 5A and LS.428 (NF.389) 5B in the markings applied for the film *Sink the Bismarck./Fleet Air Arm Museum*

Left: Swordfish II HS.158 out over Yorkshire having its picture taken prior to being delivered to the Fleet Air Arm. All Swordfish built by the Blackburn company were known as Blackfish./*Hawker Siddeley Aviation*

Introduction

In the great Valhalla of the skies, next to the hall of fame of slain warriors, is one for aircraft and sharing honours with the greatest is — the Fairey Swordfish.

This biplane with a legendary history and achievements second to none, had the affection of all who flew it, in peace or war. Known universally as the 'Stringbag' it defied efforts to replace it with more modern equipment and served in front line squadrons of the Fleet Air Arm from 1936 to 1945. Some squadrons, Nos 813 and 825 for instance, operated it for eight and nine years respectively. At the outbreak of war 13 squadrons in the FAA were equipped with the Swordfish and at the end of hostilities there were still nine first line squadrons with them. That the aircraft was successful in its designed role there is no doubt, and for the first four years of the World War 2 fully justified the beliefs of the FAA in the carrier-based torpedo-bomber.

The discovery that it was possible to drop torpedoes from aircraft is credited to the Italians who tried it in 1911. The RNAS were not slow to see its potential and on July 28, 1914, Lt A. M. Longmore, (later Air Chief Marshal Sir Arthur Longmore) made a successful torpedo drop from a Short seaplane. In June 1915, the first Short 184s, developed specifically by Shorts for torpedo carrying, were delivered to the RNAS at Mudros for use in the Dardenelles campaign. Operating from the seaplane carrier, *Ben My Chree*, the first attack was made on August 12, 1915, when Flight Commander C. H. K. Edmonds glided down to within 300 yards of his target and scored a hit. On August 17 the same officer made another attack on a convoy of three vessels, hitting a steamer which was set on fire and subsequently sunk. Flt Lt G. B. Dacre sank a tug but it could hardly be claimed as an aerial attack as he made his release while taxi-ing across the water after an engine failure! The first torpedoes were 14-inch, weighing 850lbs, but these were replaced by the 1 086lb mark. It was found that this model was still too light to inflict serious damage and in late 1917 the Admiralty were looking for an aircraft capable of carrying the Mk VIII, 1 423lb torpedo which had a fifty per cent bigger warhead.

The Sopwith Aviation Company were approached in 1916 to develop a torpedo-bomber and the result was the Sopwith T.1 Cuckoo. This entered service in July 1918 and was capable of carrying the new Mk IX 18-inch torpedo. By now the RAF — which had absorbed the RNAS — was well ahead of the rest of the world in the field, both in performance and experience. During the inter-war years Blackburn produced most of the torpedo-bombers with types such as the Swift, Ripon, Baffin and Shark. Later Fairey entered the field with the Swordfish and followed it with the Albacore and Barracuda. However, the monoplane torpedo aircraft never made an operational strike and it fell to the biplanes to make the last torpedo attack in the war. Interest in the aerial torpedo did not lapse however, the 1944 specification which resulted in the Westland Wyvern was for a torpedo-strike-fighter and was in evidence in the early fifties. In more recent times the Fairey Gannet and certain types of helicopter became the launching platforms for the modern homing torpedo.

The last classic torpedo attack by Swordfish was the tragic but gallant attempt by six aircraft from No 825 Squadron when they tried to sink the German warships *Prinz Eugen*, *Scharnhorst* and *Gneisenau*. After this they were relegated to the anti-submarine role with depth charges. However, the Swordfish was a pioneer in two other fields that were to give it a new lease of life. The first was air-to-surface (ASV) radar and the second was rocket projectiles. First trials with ASV were disappointing but a break through was made on December 26, 1939. The Swordfish III had ASV built into it and from late 1941 was used on operations. In fact on December 21, 1941, a Swordfish of No 812 Squadron based at Gibralter sank the first U-boat to be destroyed by an aircraft at night. The first rocket projectiles fired by the Swordfish was on October 12, 1942, at Thorney Island, and although a Hurricane had test-fired them a year before, it fell to the Swordfish to evaluate the new weapon for FAA work. Combining ASV with R/P made a formidable weapon system, even in a slow aircraft like the Swordfish. Thus, when the Swordfish went to sea in escort carriers or MAC ships, the U-boats found it more and more difficult to operate. Later, when fighters were formed into composite squadrons with Swordfish for anti-submarine strike teams it was entirely successful. The tactics adopted were that the fighters, usually Wildcats, would be at readiness on the flight deck and when the Swordfish sent in a sighting report they would scramble. Then the Swordfish would go in with R/P, bombs or depth charges while the fighters strafed the U-boats gun mounts. The Swordfish crews, more than in any other type during World War 2, had to operate in all weather conditions in an open cockpit and as such frequently had a bond of camaraderie which was unsurpassed. On Arctic routes the weather was appalling, temperatures below freezing, spray and snow freezing as it fell, usually six inches of snow on the flight decks, very heavy sea swells, thick cloud and visibility less than half a mile was common. Serviceability remained high and crews out on patrols often found it a gamble on whether they would get back, and when they did, had to be lifted, frozen, from the cockpits. A blind-landing device which employed a beacon on the carrier responding to aircraft ASV signals (BABS) was fitted to the carriers but soon proved of limited use because of the yaw of the ship. Interestingly, No 825 Squadron evolved a talk-down system in 1944 which worked and became the first talk down ever used on a carrier. One of the Swordfish PPI scanners was installed on the starboard quarter of the ship and operated by the squadron Air Radio Officer from his workshop, which was also on the starboard quarter and just below the flight deck. The two mile range scale on the scope was used with the centre spot expanded out to the one mile circle, this was drawn to the bottom of the screen and gave a high degree of accuracy at very short range. At sea in poor visibility it proved of inestimable value.

The Swordfish was, of course, just an aeroplane, its legends, its achievements, were only as good as the skilled and gallant crews could make them.

Top right: An unusual view of the last preserved Swordfish LS.326 seen here on May 28, 1964 on the occasion of the Fleet Air Arm Review at Yeovilton. Flown by Rear Admiral P. D. Gick with two other crew members who had all flown together some 25 years before (combined ages totalled over 150 years), Rear Admiral H. R. V. Janvrin and Lt Cdr C. Topliss. As the Swordfish flew past the reviewer, in this case, HRH Prince Phillip, the crew stood up and saluted. This caused some amusement and the idea has been used ever since as part of the display programme which the aircraft puts on around the country during the year./*Royal Navy*

Right: A fine study of Swordfish V.4719 K over the California countryside on June 1, 1942. A number of Swordfish were used from time to time to go with British carriers to the USA when they needed repairs. The Swordfish provided anti-submarine patrols./*Navy Department*

4

Birth of a TSR

If anyone can lay claim to the origins of the Fairey Swordfish, it must surely be the Greek Naval Air Arm. For a number of years they had been flying Fairey IIIF Mk.IIIB three-seat spotter reconnaissance aircraft and it was only to be expected that they should approach the Fairey Aviation Co Ltd when they wished to replace them.

After talks, a specification was drawn up and finally issued in July 1932 to the Fairey Technical Department for a Greek naval torpedo bomber, and this was to form the basic operational requirement that was eventually to result in the Swordfish.

The general requirement was that the aircraft must fulfil three primary naval duties; (a) Fleet reconnaissance with a crew of three; (b) torpedo attacks with a crew of two and of limited range, and (c) bombing attacks with two or three crew according to bomb load. The design was to allow conversion from landplane to floatplane as required with the structure capable of withstanding catapulting and arresting loads as laid down in contemporary British Air Ministry practice. A moderately-supercharged Rolls-Royce Kestrel engine was specified but design had to allow easy conversion to alternative water-cooled or air-cooled types — a fortuitous requirement in this case as the Kestrel was later replaced by an air-cooled type. Dimensions, which were not to be exceeded, were for a 46 foot span, reduced to 18 feet when folded; 37 feet fuselage length and 14 feet nine inches in height. Enough

fuel and oil were required for an eight hour sortie at cruising speed at 8 000 feet. The maximum speed at this altitude was to be 140 knots with an alighting speed of 50 knots. With the torpedo or bombs the maximum speed was not to be less than 133 knots. Fixed armament was to be one machine gun in the forward fuselage with 600 rounds of ammunition. The observer was to have a Lewis gun with six drums of ammunition. Provision was to be made for carrying a light, 1 500lb, torpedo, depth charges, two 500lb or four 100lb bombs. Other requirements were for modern up to date instrumentation, night flying equipment, W/T and R/T wireless and buoyancy apparatus. A design to meet these requirements was drawn up by Marcel Lobelle, a domiciled Belgian who was at that time chief designer for the Fairey Aviation Co. The design was known as the Fairey PV Ship-plane (TSR) and was allotted the Fairey factory number F.1875. Fairey were already at work on a British fleet spotter reconnaissance aircraft to specification S.9/30, the contract to proceed with a prototype being received on August 3, 1931. They had also submitted design studies to the earlier specification M.1/30 which had been for a two-seat torpedo bomber. There was a strong resemblance between the aircraft to meet all three requirements and Fairey realised clearly that the wide range of naval military requirements the Greek design offered might well make it suitable for the Fleet Air Arm. Thus, in January 1933, they submitted details of the private venture machine to the Air Ministry, then still responsible for all naval air matters. While the Air Ministry were considering this new project a few changes had been made to the specification. The Kestrel had been replaced by an Armstrong Siddeley 625hp moderately-supercharged Panther VI engine with 14 cylinders in two rows. A number of minor changes were incorporated, the bomb load being increased to three 500lb bombs, one being carried centrally under the fuselage. Dunlop wheel

brakes were to be included, as was a large buoyancy twin float undercarriage which was required to be quickly interchangeable with a land undercarriage.

The PV TSR received the go-ahead and was flown for the first time with a land undercarriage from Harmondsworth aerodrome, not far from the present London Heathrow Airport, on March 21, 1933. The pilot was Flt Lt Chris Staniland, then chief test pilot for the Fairey concern. Shortly after the first flight, the Air Ministry informed Fairey that they were issuing specification S.15/33 which was intended to cover the construction of a general-purpose aircraft for the FAA, substantially combining the previously published requirements of M.1/30 and S.9/30 except for modifications as laid down. In fact, apart from the power plant, which could be of any British approved engine, and provided that the aircraft conformed with the stated requirements for the torpedo bomber, of which the gross weight when flying should not exceed 7 500lb, the design was much the same as Fairey's submission to the Air Ministry. The gross weight was important because ships' catapults were not capable of launching aircraft with an all up weight exceeding 8 000lb. After preliminary flying trials the Panther VI was changed in June to a 635hp Bristol Pegasus IIM nine-cylinder radial engine driving a Watts two-blade wooden propeller. It was flown for the first time in this form by Flt Lt Staniland on July 10, 1933. It now featured spatted wheels and later, an arrestor hook was fitted to the rear fuselage in anticipation of service trials. Although generally referred to previously as the TSR.1 there is no evidence to show that this appendage was used until a second machine was being built and this was called the TSR II to avoid confusion. In fact, in surviving Fairey and Air Ministry documentation it is constantly referred to as the Fairey S.15/33 or PV TSR.

Left: A rear view of the PV. TSR powered here by an Armstrong Siddeley Panther engine driving a two-blade metal propeller. The engine is devoid of the Townend ring with which it was fitted later. Note the more pointed fin and rudder and the large crew cockpit.

Top: The PV.TSR again after being fitted with a Bristol Pegasus IIM engine, spats and an arrestor hook for expected service trials. In the background, a Fairey IIIF.

Above: A little known picture of TSR.II K.4190 shortly after it was assembled at the Great West Aerodrome at Heathrow. This was the private Fairey airfield now absorbed into London Airport Heathrow./*Fairey Aviation*

Above: K.4190 after being sprayed up in Service markings and rolled out for test flying.

Centre left: A head on view of K.4190 showing the clean lines before it started to get cluttered with bombs, depth charges, mines, torpedoes, rockets and ASV.

Bottom left: November 1934 and K.4190 is lifted off Hamble water for a test flight. It was stressed for catapult launching and subsequently completed catapult launching trials aboard HMS *Repulse./Real Photographs*

Top right: August 1937 and K.4190 is fitted with dual control after a crash a year before and a complete re-build.

Thus, the Greeks now having lost interest in the proceedings, development work and test flying continued at a satisfactory pace, until September 11, 1933. On this day Staniland was doing spinning trials at different loadings but was having difficulty persuading the aircraft to go into the spin. Then, at 14 000 feet, with slots unlocked, he initiated a right hand spin which, without any warning became very flat with the nose well up and fast rotation. The normal recovery actions, including opening the throttle, merely caused the TSR to shake violently. After some 12 turns Staniland decided to abandon recovery — and the aircraft. He elected to leave the left side of the cockpit as the spin was to the

right expecting to be thrown clear. His first attempt however was foiled by 'g' and the airflow and he found himself deposited in the rear cockpit. He succeeded in his second attempt. The TSR finally crashed at Longford in Middlesex.

After the inquiry, all the departments involved with the TSR such as design, experimental, drawing office, technical and flight test, were invited to submit proposals for a second experimental aircraft. This was done during September 25/26, 1933 and the overall general theme was that the policy should be one of development rather than radical re-design. It was suggested that small improvements could be made in a number of places which would lead to simplicity, ease of maintenance and generally make a much better aircraft. The extent to which the original design could be repeated depended on whether an acceptable cure could be found for the flat spin. Staniland reported that although certain modifications had been carried out to the tailplane prior to the crash there was still a certain amount of tail buffeting at slow speeds with a tendancy to fore and aft instability. He also suggested that a three-blade propeller would improve performance as it was much superior to the two-blade type. The experimental department asked for some 78 minor improvements to be incorporated. A decision to build a second PV TSR was made shortly after the enquiry.

The second aircraft built to S.15/33 was known as the TSR.II and allotted serial number K.4190 for service trials. It was externally similar to the earlier TSR design but incorporated an extra bay into the fuselage. (Much of the re-design work was undertaken by H. E. Chaplin, who later became chief designer and responsible for the 'droop snoot' of the Fairey FD.2) A longer fuselage was compensated for by a four-degree sweepback on the upper wings. Anti-spin strakes were added to the rear fuselage

just forward of the tailplane leading edges. The fin and rudder had a greater chord but construction, although differing in small detail, was generally similar to the earlier TSR. The engine was changed to a more powerful 690hp Bristol Pegasus IIIM3 nine-cylinder radial with a wide chord Townend ring affixed at seven points. Initially a Watts two-blade wooden propeller was fitted but later a two-blade metal, and finally a three-blade Fairey-Reed metal propeller was used. K.4190 was flown for the first time by Chris Staniland from the private Fairey airfield known as the Great West Aerodrome, (now London Heathrow Airport) on April 17, 1934. During the contractors' trials lasting some two months, 91 further minor installation and modifications were carried out before K.4190 left for Martlesham Heath in June 1934.

In those days all civil and military aircraft were tested at the Aeroplane and Armament Experiment Establishment at Martlesham Heath both for trials and suitability to role. One of the pilots conducting the trials was Flt Lt Duncan Menzies who later found himself employed by Fairey as a test pilot checking out production Swordfish. The eventual trials report in general was favourable toward the TSR.II but some criticism was made of the slow recovery from spins, stalling features and the longitudinal instability in dives with an aft CG position. The controls were judged to be light and effective though the ailerons snatched at the stall and in spins. The rudder was heavy and with slots free at the stall it would not stop the tendency to roll. Spins were carried out with ballasted weights up to 7 500lb to represent a torpedo load. Dives at speeds up to 210 knots indicated were made without any vibrations and were steady except for aft CG positions when there was a certain amount of fore and aft instability. This trouble was cured with changes in elevator move-

9

ment ranges. K.4190 then went to the Royal Aircraft Establishment at Farnborough for preliminary catapult trials and then on to HMS *Courageous* for deck landing trials. In November it went to the Fairey factory at Hamble for floatplane tests. On November 10, Staniland flew the initial test with twin floats and subsequently K.4190 completed catapult floatplane trials from HMS *Repulse*. On January 1, 1935, the aircraft went to the Marine Aircraft Experimental Establishment at Felixstowe to be examined from the repair and maintenance point of view. The conclusion — correct as events were to prove — was that there would be no difficulty with the repair and maintenance of TSR.II aircraft in service. K.4190 then went on to the Torpedo Trials Unit at Gosport where it crashed in February 1935, was sent back to Fairey and underwent a complete rebuild before emerging in January 1936. It was tested again in April with modified ailerons and in July with modified oleo legs and a larger diameter tail wheel. Similar test flights were carried out for the rest of 1936 and early 1937. The aircraft underwent modification in July and on August 18 Staniland started testing the dual controls that had been fitted. On September 6, 1937, K.4190 finally joined the FAA at Gosport. After use by the station flight and A Flight, K.4190 was struck off charge exactly one year from the date of delivery — September 6, 1938.

At the same time as K.4190 emerged rebuilt in January 1936, three other development aircraft emerged — K.5660, K.5661 and K.5662. With the success of K.4190 in its trials the Air Ministry, on April 23, 1935, issued specification S.38/34 which called for three development aircraft to be built from the drawings of K.4190 in its final form and for these aircraft and the subsequent production machines, to be known as — *Swordfish*.

Top: A first class shot of K.4190 over Middlesex in May 1934. At this time it still had a two-blade propeller./*Flight*

Right: The late Chris Staniland demonstrating the TSR.II K.4190 at Fairey's Great West Aerodrome. Note the anti-spin strakes just forward of the tailplane. The aircraft in the background is K.1695, the prototype Fairey Hendon bomber./*Flight*

Production

At the same time that the three pre-production aircraft were ordered the Air Ministry also issued an order for 86 Mk1 Swordfish, followed by another for 131. Production quickly got under way at the Hayes factory with one aircraft being turned out in 1935, 147 in 1936, 201 in 1937, 143 in 1938, 197 in 1939 and three in 1940 when production was handed over to Blackburn to make way at Hayes for the successor to the Swordfish — the Albacore.

Blackburn had been approached when it became obvious Fairey would not be able to turn Swordfish out in sufficient numbers due to other production commitments. The Admiralty Director of Air Materiel, Captain M. S. (later Rear Admiral Sir Matthew) Slattery suggested Blackburn should take over all Swordfish production. Although Blackburn were similarly loaded with production work it was agreed that the plan of setting up a new production centre in Yorkshire had the advantage of reduced bomb risk under the dispersal programme and spread the war load. By the end of 1940 the new production plant had been set up at Sherburn-in-Elmet between Leeds and Selby. The first Blackburn built Swordfish, V.4288, was test flown by F. H. Dixon, a Fairey test pilot, on December 1, 1940. Thereafter Blackburn produced 415 in 1941, 271 in 1942, 592 in 1943 and 420 in 1944 when production ended. The last Swordfish built was NS.204 which was rolled out in December 1944. Thus the total number of Swordfish built was 692 by Fairey and 1699 by Blackburn, 2391 in total. Serials were allotted for 2392 aircraft but for some unknown reason one Swordfish was not built. It has not so far been possible to determine which one. Unofficially the Blackburn produced aircraft were known as Blackfish and both Fairey test pilots and experienced FAA pilots claimed they could tell the difference when flying them.

Following the basic MkI Swordfish came the MkII with L.7678 as the trials aircraft. This model had a strengthened lower wing with metal skin under-surfaces for rocket projectile launching. In the same year the MkIII came out and apart from the strengthened lower wings it had 'built in' air-to-surface (ASV) Mk X radar in a radome between the undercarriage legs. Some Mk II Swordfish sent to Canada were modified to have an enclosed cockpit and these were known as Mk IVs.

There was no real problem in building the Swordfish. The fuselage was a rectangular steel-tube structure faired to oval section and covered forward with quickly detachable panels and aft of this by fabric. Large inspection panels were provided in the fabric covering. The wings were built up of two steel strip spars, steel drag struts and duralumin ribs, the whole covered in fabric. The duralumin framed ailerons were also fabric covered, one to each wing. There was one set of struts to each outer wing which folded back. The upper centre-section was carried on a pyramid structure with the lower centre-section stubs braced to upper fuselage longerons by inverted-V struts. The tail unit was of steel and duralumin with fabric covering. Each unit of the undercarriage consisted of an oleo shock-absorber leg, the upper end being anchored to the extremity of the front spar of the lower centre-section, with the lower end hinged to the fuselage by axle and forwardly inclined radius rod. The wheels, fully inter-

changeable with twin floats, had pneumatic brakes. Armament ran to a Vickers gun mounted on the front fuselage and firing through the airscrew while in the rear cockpit the gunner had a Lewis gun on a Fairey high-speed gun-mounting.

Top left: Swordfish I K.6009 in pristine condition. Photographed at Fairey's Great West Aerodrome it was first flown on 12 September, 1936 by Flt Lt. Dixon, one of the Fairey test pilots. It was delivered to No 2 Aircraft Storage Unit, then the Fleet Air Arm Pool at Gosport before joining No 822 Squadron.

Centre left: Two Swordfish Is V.4319 and V.4320 awaiting collection at the Blackburn factory at Sherburn-in-Elmet in Yorkshire./*Hawker Siddeley Aviation*

Above left: NS.204 the last Swordfish to be completed taxies away in December 1944, ten years after the flight of the first./*Hawker Siddeley Aviation*

Top right: A fine shot of Blackburn built Swordfish II HS.158 showing the rocket rails and blast plates. Note also the different exaust pipe from the Swordfish I/*Hawker Siddeley Aviation*

Right: Swordfish ribs being turned out in one of the dispersed Blackburn factories. Female workers were widely used and in other factories constituted as much as 80 per cent of the labour force./*Hawker Siddeley Aviation*

Above: Swordfish mainplanes being assembled in one of the Blackburn factories./*Hawker Siddeley Aviation*

Centre right: Swordfish fuselages take shape in the final assembly shop at the Sherburn-in-Elmet factory/*Hawker Siddeley Aviation*

Bottom right: Now the engines are being fitted. A good view of the exhaust pipes and oil cooler./*Hawker Siddeley Aviation*

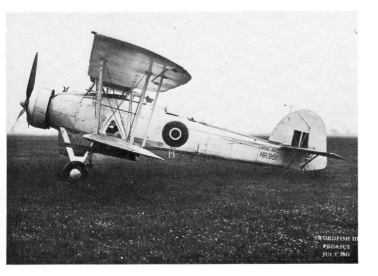

Above: Swordfish IIIs nearing completion at the Blackburn factory at Sherburn. The ASV radomes, yet to be fitted, are on the right of the picture. Between February 24 and August 18, 1944 Blackburn built 320 Swordfish IIIs./*Hawker Siddeley Aviation*

Centre left: Frontal view of Swordfish II taken in July 1944 showing the early Yagi aerials on the outer struts, and the rockets rails./*via R. C. Jones*

Bottom left: A standard Swordfish III NR.951 as taken in 1944. Most of the MkIIIs went to squadrons embarked on escort carriers./*IWM*

Halcyon Days

Above left: Superb illustration of a Swordfish leaving the catapult at Gosport, March 2, 1939. All TSR pilots underwent a required number of such launches as part of their training./*Fox Photos*

Left: Swordfish L.2824 ascends from the depths of HMS *Argus*, December 1938. This aircraft and L.2816 are being readied for trials and later flew out over the Channel. Note the RAF fitter in cockpit. At this time ground/deck crews still had a mixture of RAF and RN personnel. This continued until shortly after the war started when all deck parties were RN./*Fox Photos*

Above right: Full of the joys of flying between cloud banks, a bit of formation flying and then back to base for tea! These Swordfish are from the Torpedo Training Unit at Gosport and were snapped sometime in 1937. Aircraft, front to rear are: K.8425 E; K.8874 K, K.8872 H, K.8424 D, K.8348 C./*Ministry of Defence*

Right: Another view of the Swordfish from the TTU at Gosport. The Peggies are almost audible./*Ministry of Defence*

17

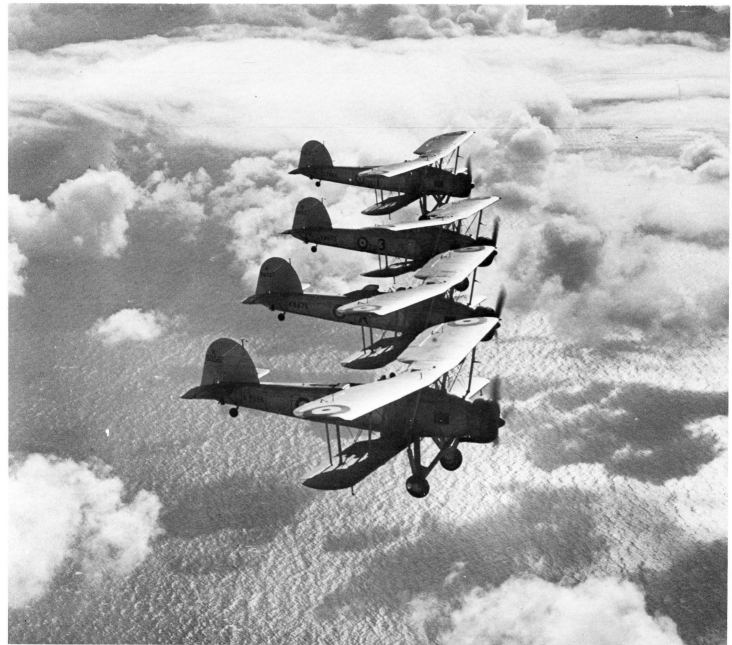

Top left: Formation practice for the TSR Course at Gosport TTU. Taken mid-1937 these have a mixture of letters and numerals. Front to rear they are-L.2727 7; L.2728 8; K. 5965 4; K.8875 K; K.8873 3; L.7651 B; K.6007 L; L.7650 I; and K.8424 D. K.8875 was a dual control aircraft and was still being used by No 785 Squadron at Crail in early 1943./*IWM*

Top Centre: Vic formation — go! The same formation of nine aircraft from the TTU Gosport. Formation flying was an important part of a pilots training./*IWM*

Left: K.5956; K.8875 A; K.8873 3; and L.7650 I practise formation flying over the sea./*IWM*

Centre right, above: No 820 Squadron in formation off the Scottish coast probably September 1938 when the Swordfish squadrons from *Ark Royal* flew to Evanton for their annual weapon training. 648 is K.8880, the leader is L. 2720 and 647 is K.8881

Top right: Taken at Sealand in 1938 this shot of K.6009 912 is unusual because Fleet Air Arm squadrons rarely went in for chequered marking and this one has fin and wing tips so marked. The squadron badge on the fin is of No 822 Squadron which were based at Gosport and joined *Furious* for embarked flying./*Ministy of Defence*

Centre right, below: Flying low over the sea are K.8402 580 and K.8399 583 of No 813 Squadron from HMS*Eagle.* The fuselage band is black as is the flight commander's fin on 580./*via R. C. Jones*

Bottom right: A formation of Swordfish from No 824 Squadron from HMS *Eagle.* Black fuselage bands and fin colours, the furthest away having no fin marking, the next one K.8367 948 has one black band, K.8386 945 has an all black fin being the flight commander's aircraft, and K.8391 952 has black/white/black on the fin./*via R. C. Jones*

A well known picture of No 814 Squadron with *Ark Royal* in the background.

Spectator fashion helps to capture the atmosphere of the pre-war era in this shot of K.5949.

Swordfish K.8869 parked on the grass at Hamble sometime in 1937.

Top right: A well known picture of No 814 Squadron with *Ark Royal* in the background. Swordfish are L.9771 705; L.9774 708; L.9777 701; L.9779 702; L.2764 710; and L.2733 703. The three fuselage bands are blue/red/blue./*via R. C. Jones*

Centre right, above: Spectator fashion helps to capture the atmosphere of the pre-war era in this shot of K.5949 taken at the Fairey Great West Aerodrome on May 10, 1936. The occasion was the annual Royal Aeronautical Society Garden Party, sponsored for many years by Sir Richard Fairey. K.5949 was delivered to Lee-on-Solent on October 2, 1936 by Sergeant Tingley where it served with C Flight and later A Flight./*A. J. Jackson*

Centre right, below: Swordfish K.8869 parked on the grass at Hamble sometime in 1937. It was first flown on April 17 and delivered to RAF Cardington by Sgt Gifford on April 27. It was still around in early 1941 when it was in use at Dekheila with the Pool Squadron./*A. J. Jackson*

Below: All TSR pilots took a seaplane course at Calshot where they learned to handle the floatplanes of the day. From 1936 this meant the Swordfish and K.5992 has a dual control floatplane seen here on Empire Air Day at Calshot in 1937. It was struck off charge in April 1939./*A. J. Jackson*

Far right, top: Swordfish floatplane L.2742 529 of No 701 Catapult Flight in flight near Gibraltar in 1938. From January 1940 all the Catapult Flights were pooled under No 700 Squadron./*Charles E. Brown*

Far right, bottom: With the engine still running this Swordfish floatplane K.8369 is hoisted aboard. The battleship in the background appears to be HMS *Malaya .*/*Charles E. Brown*

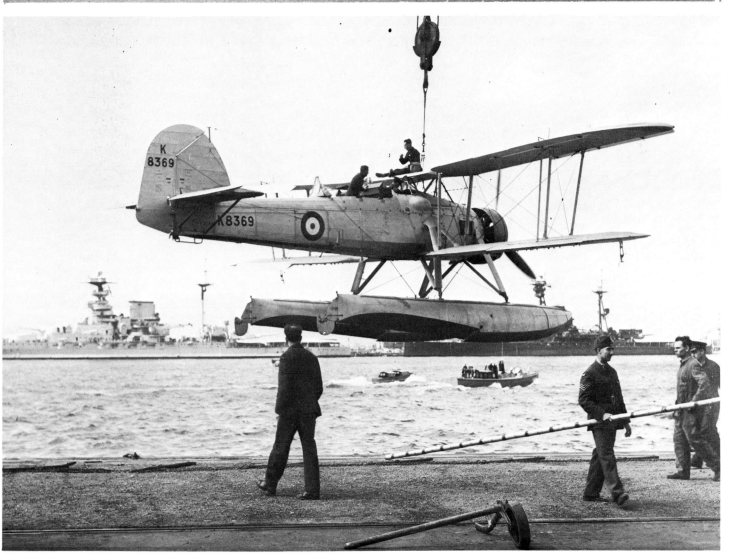

How to drop a 'fish

Left: Another torpedo delivery this time from Swordfish L.7651 B into the Solent off Calshot. Torpedo attacks were usually made from forward of the beam at a range of about 900 yards. The art was in aiming off to allow for the ship's movement during the torpedo's running time. A primitive sight was fitted to the Swordfish to allow for this./*IWM*

Top right: One of the few photographs available of a wartime training torpedo drop. Swordfish 5F shown here is from No 785 Squadron based at Crail./*via R. C. Jones*

Centre right: Swordfish F of an unidentified unit flying along the coast carrying a parachute sea mine./*IWM*

Below: A rare view of Swordfish 22 making a wartime practice torpedo drop. When dropped at 1 000 yards range it took 40 to 50 seconds to reach its target. Practice torpedoes were set to run at a depth sufficient to pass safely underneath the target and the warhead was buoyant so that the torpedo could be recovered./*Fleet Air Arm Museum*

Taranto

When war with Germany and Italy seemed inevitable in 1938, the Commander-in-Chief of the British Mediterranean Fleet, Admiral Sir Dudley Pound, requested Captain A. L. St G Lyster, commanding the carrier *Glorious* to draw up plans for attacking the Italian Fleet in Taranto harbour with his highly trained TBR squadrons. In fact, a plan along these lines had been drawn up in 1935 and using this as a basis Commanders G. Willoughby and L. Mackintosh, respectively the Senior FAA Officer and Senior Observer aboard the *Glorious* set about a new plan. The ship's three TBR squadrons were to spearhead the attack at night with 12 Swordfish each. These were Nos 812, 823 and 825 Squadrons. Necessary to ensure success were timely reconnaissance, night flying training, an undetected approach to the fly-off position, — and a certain amount of luck. When war did break out the *Glorious* was required elsewhere and on April 10, 1940, she sailed for home to take part in the ill-fated Allied Expeditionary Force to Norway. A new carrier, HMS *Illustrious* was sent to the Mediterranean in her place. On board she had Nos 815 and 819 Squadrons with Swordfish and No 806 with the new Fulmar.

A revised plan was drawn up for an attack on Trafalgar Day-October 21, 1940. Some 30 Swordfish were to make the attack in two waves of 15 aircraft. Nine Swordfish in each wave would carry torpedoes and six would carry bombs. A few days before the raid, however, near tragedy struck. A gunner working on one of the Swordfish slipped and his screwdriver struck a pair of exposed terminals causing a spark. The aircraft hangar on a carrier is confined at the best of times and on this day the atmosphere was saturated in petrol fumes. The spark touched off a flash which developed into an explosion, disintegrating the tailplane of the Swordfish. Flames spread quickly but the situation was soon in hand although not one Swordfish out of the two squadrons was fit to fly. Apart from two which were complete write-offs all the rest had to be taken up to the flight deck to be thoroughly washed out with fresh water. Engines, instruments and wireless sets had to be completely stripped down, cleaned, dried and re-assembled. It was obvious the attack could not be launched as planned and a new date was fixed for the night of October 30/31. However there was no moon that night and the raid was postponed again. It had been intended that HMS *Eagle* would combine forces with the *Illustrious* for the operation but she developed defects in her petrol system and after transferring five Swordfish and eight crews to the *Illustrious* she sailed for Alexandria. The next night suitable for the attack was the night of November 11 and plans went ahead. An RAF reconnaissance during the 11th revealed that the Italian Fleet were in harbour including no less than six battleships. At 6pm that evening the C-in-C detached the *Illustrious* with an escort of four cruisers and four destroyers to the fly-off position. Wireless operator air gunners were not carried and this meant that internal auxiliary fuel tanks could be fitted in the rear cockpit to enhance the range. The first strike force of 12 Swordfish was made up of six armed with torpedoes, four with bombs and two with flares and bombs. This was because the harbour was protected by balloons and nets as well as 22 anti-aircraft gun positions. The plan was for the torpedo Swordfish to attack the battleships lying in the outer harbour, and as a diversion the bombers were to make a synchronised attack on the crusiers and destroyers alongside the inner harbour quay.

The strike force, led by Lt Cdr K. Williamson with Observer Lt N. J. Scarlett in Swordfish L4A formed up eight miles from HMS *Illustrious* and set course at 2057. Flying conditions were good and the Swordfish cruising along at 75 knots IAS expected no trouble on the 170 mile trip to Taranto. At 2115, however, the squadron became separated in cloud and eventually four of the Swordfish had to attack independently. The flare-droppers were detached at 2256, the first laying a line of flares along the eastern side of the harbour. This aircraft, with the other flare droppers then made a dive bombing attack on an oil storage depot and set it on fire. The first sub-flight of three Swordfish made its attack from 4 000 feet although by the time they released their torpedoes they were down to 400 feet. Lt Cdr Williamson released his torpedo at the *Cavour* and this made a hit, the gunfire from the ship unfortunately shooting him down to become, with his observer, a POW. Sub Lt P. Sparke, DSC, in L4C with Sub Lt J. Neale as observer saw his torpedo strike a *Cavour* class ship before climbing safely into the darkness. Sub Lt A. Macauley with Observer Sub Lt T. Wray were in L4R and they also released their torpedo at the *Cavour*. L4K flown by Lt N. Kemp with observer Sub Lt R. Bailey led in the second wave and attacked the *Littorio*. Lt H. Swayne with observer Lt J. Buscall in L4M also attacked the *Littorio* before turning round and streaking back the way he had come. E4F one of the *Eagle* Swordfish flown by Lt Maund with Sub Lt W. Bull as observer, also attacked the *Littorio*. Captain O. Patch, a Royal Marine pilot flying another *Eagle* Swordfish, E5A with Sub Lt D. Goodwin as observer, had as their task the bombing of the cruisers and destroyers. Patch attacked from 1 500 feet dropping his bombs as he flew over the cruisers at mast level. L4L was flown by Sub Lt B. Sarra with Sub Lt J. Bowker as observer and they bombed the seaplane base, scoring a direct hit on a hangar. Last of the first wave bombers was Sub Lt T. Forde in L4H with Sub Lt A. Mardel-Ferreira as observer. Diving from 1 500 feet Forde let one salvo of bombs go at the cruisers but unsure of the results he calmly went round again. Meanwhile, the two flare-dropping Swordfish, L4P flown by Lt L. Kiggell with H. Janvrin as observer, and L5B piloted by Lt C. Lamb with Grieve of the *Eagle's* 813 Squadron as observer. These two, after dropping their flares successfully watched the main action and when this had finished, dived to bomb the oil storage depot behind Cape San Vito but saw no results. There was a lull, the first strike was over after only 23 minutes of action.

The second strike force of nine Swordfish began taking off from HMS *Illustrious* at 2123. This force was led by Lt Cdr J. W. Hale in L5A with Lt G. A. Carline as observer. Five were to attack with torpedoes, two with bombs and two with flares and bombs. While taxi-ing along the flight deck the eighth Swordfish collided with the last machine and had to be struck down for repairs. The observer, Lt G. R. M. Going, asked the Captain for permission to follow the strike when repairs were completed and this was granted, this Swordfish taking off 24 minutes after the rest. L5Q flown by Lt S. Morford with observer Sub Lt R. Green lost its auxiliary fuel tank when the straps securing it parted. The engine cut at the same time but Lt Morford managed to regain control and eventually landed back on. At 2310 the second wave sighted the glow from Taranto and expected a warm welcome. Lt Cdr Hale directed the two flare dropping Swordfish, L5B flown by Lt R. Hamilton with observer Sub Lt J. Weekes and L4F flown by Lt R. Skelton with Sub Lt E. Perkins as observer, to drop their flares. The two aircraft skimmed over the eastern shore of the Mar Grande, Lt Hamilton flying round the perimeter dropping flares at 15-second intervals, while Lt Skelton added more by depositing eight to the south-east. Both aircraft then dived to bomb the oil storage depot. Lt Cdr Hale in L5A formed the five torpedo Swordfish into line astern and flicked his navigation lights on briefly to give the signal to attack. The flak by now was terrifying, the Italians were putting up a box barrage, every gun on shore or afloat were firing upwards at a predetermined deflection and range. Hale made out a *Littorio*-class battleship and released his torpedo from 30 feet above the sea, afterwards climbing away into the darkness. L5H with Lt C. Lea as pilot and Sub Lt J. Jones as observer released their torpedo at a *Cavour*-class battleship from less than 30 feet. Lt Torrens-Spence in L5K with observer A. Sutton was following Lt Lea and as they came over Cape Rondinella he put the Swordfish into a steep dive. In the dive L5K almost collided with E4H but he managed to avoid it to pull out at mast height and press the torpedo release. Nothing happened! He quickly re-cocked the release and pressed again. This time the torpedo went, aimed at less than 700 yards at a *Littorio*-class ship. E5H with Lt J. Wellham as pilot and Lt P Humphreys as observer was hit early on its run in. One bullet struck an outer aileron rod and Wellham had a job controlling the aircraft. He released his torpedo for an angled shot of a *Littorio*-class ship and broke away as he saw it running true. Fleeing the harbour, a 40mm shell exploded on the port wing shattering some of the wing ribs and tearing the fabric. E4H flown by Bayly with observer Slaughter, was the Swordfish that nearly collided with Torrens-Spence who had in fact seen the last few moments of that gallant crew for nothing more was heard of them. Meanwhile, some 50 miles behind the second force L5F flown by Lt Clifford with observer Lt Going came plodding on. They made a landfall five miles east of Taranto and heading north-west over the town dropped their bombs from 500 feet across two cruisers.

All the Swordfish except two returned to land on the *Illustrious* safely. A second strike planned for the following night had to be called off due to bad weather.

The full results were not known for two days but then photographs showed the *Littorio* with a heavy list and her fo'c'sle awash; the *Caio Duilio* lay with her bows aground; the *Conte di Cavour* was listing heavily to port with her stern and starboard upper deck awash and she settled on the bottom the next morning; two *Trento*-class cruisers were damaged; two fleet auxiliaries had their sterns under water and bombs and incendiaries dropped on the seaplane base and oil storage depot caused some damage, but not as much as hoped. The shore batteries fired some 13 489 rounds of ammunition at the Swordfish but there are no statistics for the ships' guns.

The raid had been a fantastic success. Captain Boyd at the time said 'It is impossible to praise too highly those who in these comparatively slow machines made studied and accurate attacks in the midst of intense anti-aircraft fire. It is hoped that this victory will be considered a suitable reward to those whose work and faith in the FAA has made it possible'.

There was disappointment in the initial awards that were made in recognition of what was probably one of the most outstanding carrier raids of the World War 2. Williamson and Hale, the strike leaders, each received the DSO, and their observers, Scarlett and Carline the DSC. Patch and Goodwin also received the DSC, and that was it! The New Year's Honour List gave Admiral Lyster the CB, Captains Boyd and Bridge of the *Illustrious* and *Eagle* respectively, the CBE. It was another six months before full recognition of the gallant attack was made, then DSO's were awarded to Clifford, Going, Kemp, Torrens-Spence, Lea, Kiggell, Macauley, Hamilton, Janvrin, Sutton, Bailey, Jones, Neale. Weekes and Wray received the DSC. Sparke a bar to his DSC and 18 others were Mentioned in Despatches. But by then the awards

were far to late, for one third of those involved in the Taranto strike were dead — killed in action.

Below: A picture of bombs on the flight deck of HMS *Illustrious* November 1940. The chalk reads — *Next Stop Taranto.*/via R. C. Jones

Centre: A view of Taranto harbour on December 15, 1940 at noon showing the *Dulio* beached./*Fleet Air Arm Museum*

Bottom: Taken two minutes after the *Dulio* shot this one shows the *Cavour* sunk in the harbour. The white effect around the ship is caused by oil leaking away./*Fleet Air Arm Museum*

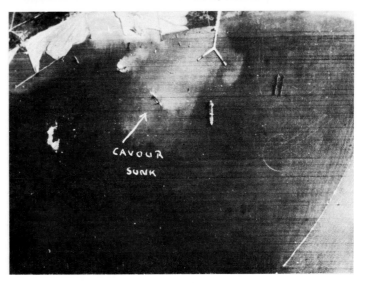

Bits of 'fish

Above: A first class view of the enclosed canopy fitted to Swordfish for use in Canada. This one is on the test aircraft HS.553 and the rear hinged section is clearly shown./*Fairey Aviation*

Centre right: Experimental fitting of a Leigh-Light under the port wing with the power pack mounted between the undercarriage legs. Although not used operationally, a pair of Swordfish acting as a hunter/killer team and equipped with ASV, rockets and a Leigh-Light could have been a deterrent to U-boats./*Fairey Aviation*

Bottom right: View of a torpedo being loaded under a Swordfish. The three-man operated winch pack is similar in style to the Aden gun pack which is fitted to the Hawker Hunter jet fighter and also requires a three-man winch team./*Fox Photos*

Left: An uncluttered view of the magnificent Pegasus IIIM3 engine. Its record of reliability was little short of fantastic.

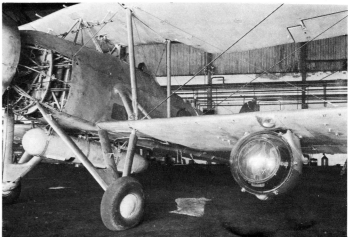

Above: The main petrol tank, oil tank, oil cooler and Browning gun.

Centre left: Front end of the Stringbag showing the collector ring and exaust, support struts and the Fairey — Reed metal fixed pitch propeller.

Bottom left: A clear view of the arrangement for the inertia starter hand gear which was one of the few faults on the Swordfish.

Top right: Pilot's cockpit of the Swordfish with the panel over the Browning gun removed. The small triangular panel is an inspection door for elevator control attachment.

Right: Tail assembly of the prototype Swordfish K.4190 showing the tailwheel and simple construction.

Far right: Observer/TAG cockpit showing the Fairey High Speed Gun Mounting with trough for the Lewis gun. The small bulges on each side of the forward part of the cockpit are bearing-compass mounts.

28

Malta Squadron

Bastion of defence that it was, the island of Malta held the key to the control of the supply routes through the Mediterranean and along the North African coastline. Despite continual efforts by the Axis air forces to bomb and starve the island into submission, it refused to give in and was subsequently awarded the George Cross for the courage and determination of its civilian and military population to carry on against all odds.

Among the military units on the island during those crucial times (1940-1943) was No 830 Squadron of the FAA equipped with Fairey Swordfish. Its origins started in 1940 when No 767 Squadron, the FAA deck landing training squadron took 24 Swordfish to Hyeres in Southern France. Planning to make better use of the weather there, they also took the old deck landing training carrier, HMS *Argus*. In the event of Italy joining Germany, the squadron was to operate under the French Admiralty for raids against Italian targets. With the end of the 'phoney war' in France a decision was made on June 10, 1940 to attack Genoa. On June 14, nine Swordfish led by Lt Cdr G. C. Dickens took off loaded with French bombs secured in place by spun yarn and fused before take off. Twenty three bombs fell on Genoa but the following night the Italians retaliated by bombing Hyères. On 17 June the squadron received orders to leave Hyères and the following day two formations of 12 Swordfish left for Bône on the North African coast. The distance was 430 miles and the flight took four hours twenty minutes, which was near the limit of endurance as they had no reserve tanks. Some of the maintenance ratings were flown across in the Swordfish but the rest went by sea. At Bône the squadron split up, the training half flying back to UK while the rest formed up under Lt Cdr F. D. Howie. He led the force via Medjez-eb-Bab to Hal Far, Malta where they joined a few RAF communications flight Swordfish to become No 830 Squadron. Six RAF WOP/AGs stayed and flew with the squadron for about eight months. Also among those selected to stay with the strike force were two FAA Petty Officer pilots, Freddie Parr and Charlie Wines.

This was unusual as rating pilots were not fully trained in operational techniques being employed in training and communications duties.

When the squadron arrived at Hal Far crews were surprised to see buses all over the airfield and landed between them much to the chagrin of anti-invasion officers. The buses had been put there to stop enemy aircraft landing. From this time on the Swordfish of No 830 Squadron never ceased to be a real thorn in the enemy's side. By the end of December, 1940 they had sunk 9 000 tons of shipping. From May to November 1941 they sank 110 000 tons of enemy shipping and damaged another 130 000 tons. In October 1941 they were joined by the Albacores of No 828 Squadron and between then and the end of 1942 the two accounted for 400 000 tons of shipping. But the record set by No 830 Squadron has never been equalled.

Returning to 1940 however, No 830 found themselves under RAF control and the first raid was against oil tanks at Augusta. On October 16, Petty Officer Wines was flying an armed reconnaissance with his observer, Lt. Wanford and air gunner Naval Airman Pickles. They became involved in a dogfight with a Cant 105 flying boat and Wines fired off all his front gun ammunition before the Cant got away at about 135 knots. On December 21 the squadron was ordered to bomb Catania airfield at Tripoli. While the defences were concentrating on the attacking Swordfish, P.O. Wines in L.7689 'B' with Cpl. Parker of the RAF as his air gunner (TAG), he glided in from the desert side and spread three 500lb HE and two sticks of incendiary bombs across a seaplane hangar. Years afterwards P.O. Wines visited the scene and found the actual nightwatchman on duty that night. He discovered he had accounted for nine flying boats and an assortment of MTB's plus a selection of other boats on the slipway. Cpl. Parker also later achieved fame as 'Sailor Parker' on Mosquitos.

Another raid was planned on enemy cruisers and destroyers sheltering in Palermo harbour, Sicily. Four flights of three set off but encountered heavy cloud and split up, ten returning to Malta. The two pilots who pushed on were — ironically — the two ratings, Barr and Wines who got through and made their attack.

On the night of March 19, 1941, the squadron was briefed to lay mines in Tripoli harbour. The normal procedure on these raids was for 4/5 Swordfish to carry mines while 2/3 others attacked gun positions etc. as a diversion. Arriving over the harbour at 4 000 feet P.O. Wines went into a steep dive pulling out at 800 feet and straddled a ship with his bombs. It should be mentioned that well into 1941 most of the Swordfish were of the 1936 variety and as such had no blind flying instruments or torpedo sights. Rating pilots were not usually trained for torpedo work but in time of war exceptions had to be made and both Barr and Wines underwent torpedo training at Kalafrana. On the night of April 12, 1941, the squadron was briefed to make a torpedo attack on a convoy consisting of two merchant ships and five destroyers. Wines carried out a classic torpedo attack on one of the merchant ships but due to heavy gunfire from the escorting destroyers had to continue on course and fly right over his target. Shot up and partially blinded by hot oil from a fractured oil tank, Wines managed to crash-land L.7689 on the beach at Hammamet in Tunisia and with his crew spent two years as a POW. Barr never made a torpedo attack and so Wines probably has the unusual distinction of being the only rating pilot in the Royal Navy to have carried out an operational torpedo attack.

Raids against enemy targets continued, three against Tripoli harbour in June, in July two enemy vessels were attacked with torpedoes and sunk, followed by two more a few nights later. On the night of September 2/3, 1941, the squadron found and attacked four Italian merchant ships being escorted by five destroyers. This convoy had been routed through the Straits of Messina and to the eastwards in an effort to avoid the aircraft on Malta. Two were hit, the *Andrea Gritti* and the *Barbaro* with the former sinking and latter getting back to Messina under tow. Another convoy left Naples on the September 10, consisting of six merchant ships and six escorting destroyers. Attacking at 0300 on the September 12 the Swordfish missed with their torpedoes because of the skilful manoeuvring of the enemy ships. Eight Blenheims then attacked with bombs, leaving the *Caffaro* crippled and on fire, but losing three aircraft to gunfire. The Swordfish attacked again and the *Nicola Odero* came to stop on fire, later blowing up.

Tragedy struck the squadron on November 11, 1941, when seven Swordfish set off with an RAF Wellington on a strike. One Swordfish returned but nothing was ever heard again of the six Swordfish or the Wellington. In December the squadron received a new C.O., Lt Cdr F. H. E. Hopkins who was to stay until April 1942. He was in action straight away, going out on a torpedo strike December 12. The target, two enemy cruisers, were sunk by destroyers before the Swordfish arrived. On December 17 a hit was obtained on a tanker bound for Tripoli and on Christmas Day mines were laid in Tripoli harbour. Armed searches at night interspersed with torpedo strikes made up most of the sorties. The enemy were now very much aware of the threat from the Malta based aircraft became very active in their efforts to stop them.

Below: An informal shot of Lt G.M.T. Osborne in the cockpit with his observer, Lt. Bibby while Sub. Lt Davies looks on. Lt Osborne and Lt Bibby sank more shipping than any other crew while serving with No 830 Squadron on Malta. Lt Osborne was awarded a DSO and DSC for his work.

Bottom: Lt Alan Downes, the senior pilot of No 830 Squadron supervising maintenance of his Swordfish. Note the sight forward of the windscreen and the long range tank in the observer's position. Lt Downes received a DSO for flying Stringbags on operations from Malta.

Nearly every night the airfield was bombed and aircraft frequently took off and landed while these raids were on. On January 23, 1942, a large enemy convoy was located consisting of four troopships, two battleships, five cruisers and no less than 27 destroyers. A strike force of nine aircraft left Malta soon after 2030 in terrible weather conditions. Heavy rainstorms mixed with a strong north-easterly wind, increasing at times to gale force. Eventually seven of the aircraft returned for various reasons, some having been in the air for over three hours. The leader, Lt Cdr Hopkins pushed on with one other Swordfish, determined to find the enemy. Some 80 miles past the position they expected to find the convoy, they eventually located it. By now however, they were well over the safety limit on petrol and as it would have taken 30 minutes to make an attack Hopkins decided to return to Malta and get together another strike force. The two Swordfish battled their way home, the storm now increasing even more in force. At 0230 he had six aircraft and set out again. Two failed to keep formation in the weather and returned. The other four carried on and later attacked the convoy, getting two hits on the 24 000 ton Lloyd-Triestino liner, *Victoria* which later sank. The Swordfish landed back after 6½ hours in the air, an hour longer than the permitted endurance. The determination and initiative of Lt Cdr Hopkins was exemplary. He had flown for 11 hours in an open cockpit biplane in near impossible weather conditions and struck a solid blow to the enemy. He received an immediate DSO.

On the nights of January 29 and 30, 1942, the squadron was out again, scoring hits on 6 000 and 8 000 ton enemy vessels. By now the squadron were down to only three or four serviceable Swordfish. Bombing had reaped its harvest. On some occasions only two Swordfish were at readiness. The task was taken over increasingly by the Albacores of No 828 Squadron but such was the attrition rate that both came under Lt Cdr. Hopkins and he operated a composite squadron. At last, in 1943, Nos 830 and 828 were relieved by No 826 Squadron. There could be no doubt as to the contribution the Swordfish and its gallant crews had made in those critical times, recognised by awards of least six DSOs, eight DSCs, seven DSMs and nine Mentions in Despatches.

With boots on....

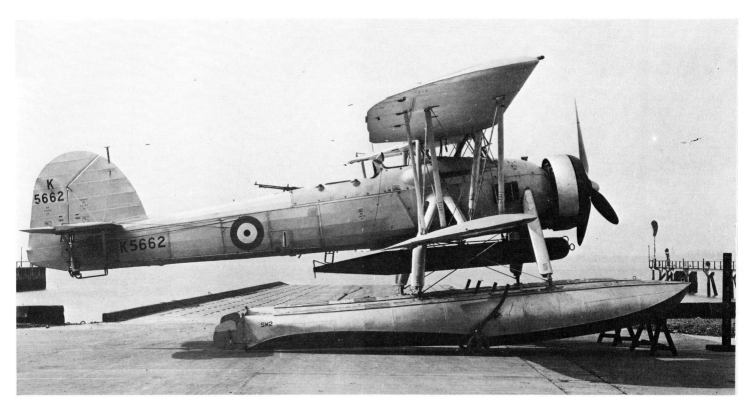

Above left: K.5662 seen here on September 5, 1936 at the Marine Aircraft Experimental Establishment at Felixstow. Complete with torpedo and Lewis gun the all up weight was around 9 000lb./*Via D. P. Woodhall*

Left: Swordfish K.5662 at Felixstowe during her trials in 1936. The twin dural floats were 26 feet 9.7 inches long and had a track of 9.8 feet./*Ministry of Defence*

Above: Seen here at speed, K.5662 at a full load was sluggish but once on the step behaviour improved until airborne. Note the amount of water being picked up./*D. Menzies*

Centre right: Three Swordfish seen here on the battleship HMS *Malaya* were (with a fourth) ferried over from the *Glorious* in September 1937. The four were required for anti-piracy patrols and were stored one in each hangar, one on trhe catapult deck and one on the catapult. Based at Mudros on the island of Lemnos at the mouth of the Dardenelles the Swordfish from *Malaya* flew a series of patrols. Apparently merchant shipping was being sunk by unidentified submarines and it was felt the Swordfish might spot something./*A. H. Trigell*

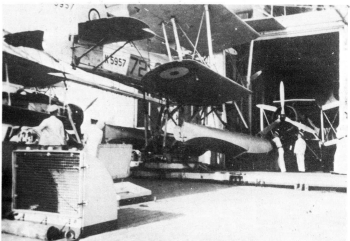

Bottom right: A view of K.5957 72 being readied on the *Malaya* for an anti-piracy patrol. They carried out this task for two months in 1937./*A. H. Trigell*

Above left: Swordfish dual floatplane K.5993 seen here at Calshot on Empire Air Day 1937. K.5993 was delivered to Calshot by Flt Lt Moneypenny on August 18, 1936./*A. J. Jackson*

Left: Unusual view of Swordfish K.5941 with wings folded and floats. It does show the relatively small storage space required for Swordfish.

Above: A peaceful run along the coast for L.7675 R5G of No 771 Squadron.

Centre right: Rare shot of three Swordfish floatplanes of No 824 Squadron on the flight deck of *Eagle.*/*via R. C. Jones*

Bottom right: K.5931 092 taxying at speed across Valetta harbour, Malta. This aircraft served with No 444 Flight at Mount Batten, 705 Flight and HMS *Repulse* before crashing on January 28, 1938 after only 310 flying hours./*via R. C. Jones*

Crews and views

Top left: At an unknown naval air station in the East African bush, a Swordfish crew prepare to go out on a anti-submarine patrol./*IWM*

Bottom left: This photograph, taken on December 5, 1940, shows just how much the TAG in the Swordfish was exposed. This aircraft and gunner were from No 812 Squadron operating with Coastal Command. Note the large extra fuel tank in the observer's position./*Fox Photo*

Top right: Home. A pilot's eye view from his Swordfish of *Ark Royal* as he flies downwind prior to landing on./*Cdr R. N. Everett*

Centre right, above: Man your aircraft! Swordfish of No 821 Squadron aboard *Ark Royal* warm up prior to some flying. In the background Skua's of No 803 Squadron./*Cdr R. N. Everett*

Centre right, below: All hands to the task. After coming up on the lift a Swordfish has its wings unfolded and is then pushed aft ready for the day's flying./*IWM*

Below: Deck party smartly manhandling Swordfish L.2731 A4G of No 820 Squadron on *Ark Royal*./*via R. C. Jones*

Top left: Sub Lts Bradford, Lett and Turnay of No 824 Squadron prepare to take off from Alexandria on an anti-submarine patrol, 1941./*Cdr S. H. SUthers*

Centre left: Deck crew rush to assist K. 8410 4C of No 813 Squadron as it bursts a tyre and swings on *Eagle's* flight deck./*Cdr S. H. Suthers*

Below: A target towing Swordfish makes a low pass over *Indomitable* in June 1942 to drop a sleeve target. A game of deck hockey is in progress./*IWM*

Right: Three of the four Swordfish that flew from Nova Scotia to San Francisco in 1942. The journey took 7½ days and involved 35½ hours flying time.

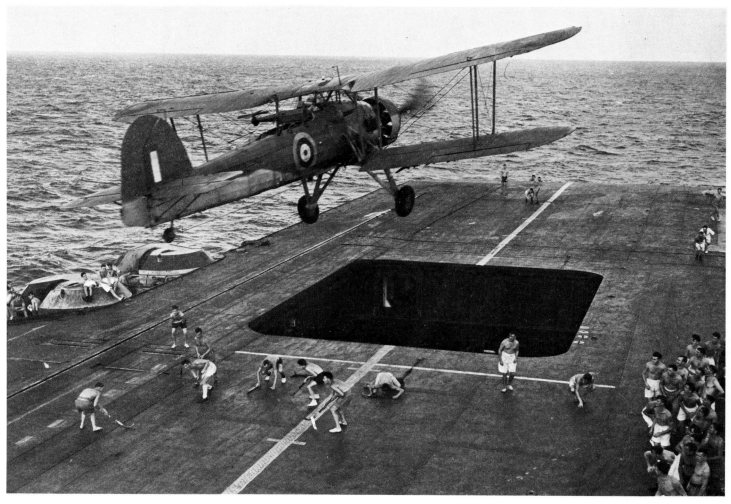

Between a cloud and a cloud
I saw you glide
in that last light, lees of the cup of day,
your good old "Peggy"* bumbling away:
the sky, and the night, and the sea beneath you, wide
and lonely, three infinities of grey.

But you had purpose, Swordfish. You were going
about your business at that steady amble
which seems so comic to those who have not seen
your shaking, snaking path when you are throwing
yourself about the sky, shell-bursts between
each bank,
or out-turning a fighter in the gamble
for hitting-space,
you fraud of a Stringbag, you.

What can you do with a Stringbag?
What *can't* you do?
You can aerobat; you can stand her on her tail;
go into a vertical dive — and pull out sweety
(you won't find the Stringbag doing a high-speed stall!).
You can take her up in any weather at all
that can be flown in,
you can trust her completely
even if visibility's next to nil,
or you have to land in a mid-Atlantic gale.
Whatever the job you give her, she will not fail—
if there are kills to be made she'll be in at the kill.
Bombing? She carries more than a Blenheim does—
and watch her spot for the guns of the Battle Fleet!
She'll torpedo a cruiser as soon as she gets the buzz,
and (you ask Doenitz!) the U-boats are her meat.

Oh, they spoil you for other aircraft for good, do Sword-
    fishes—
they've always looked obsolescent; they've never been
    obsolete;
they give a fellow the feeling of confidence and ease
like a seasoned pipe, or a dog you've trained, or old shoes
    kind to the feet.
For crews have learned to trust them who have had time
    to learn:
in long lone hours of night flight when the sky is a dry-
    point plate
as in the infinite instant of the first evasive turn
after the fish strikes water, and they open up on the crate.

Well. They've stopped producing Stringbags. And
    doubtless They know best.
I'll fly the kites they give me — and think of my earliest
    love.
They're grand are the Barracudas, and the Seafires, and
    the rest,
but — I know what the Psalmist meant, now, when he sighed
    for the wings of a dove.
And after the war is over, when the Brave New World
    appears
with planes to suit all pockets, and a seat in a sky-train's
    cheap
if I cannot purchase a Stringbag to solace my latter years —
as, once, men took to a bathchair, perhaps I'll take to
    a jeep.   R. C. S.

*"Peggy" — affectionate nickname for the Bristol Pegasus engine
which powers the Fairey Swordfish.

Reproduced from PUNCH, dated 27/9/44

A superb plan view of a Swordfish flying low over a sunlit
sea./*Navy Department*

Esmonde VC

During World War II there were many brave and courageous deeds on all sides and amongst them stands the magnificent raid by a small number of naval aviators who, in obsolescent biplanes took on the might of the German Navy and the Luftwaffe.

It began in 1941 when the British combined operations commando raid on Vaagso, an island off the Norwegian coast, along with a diversionary raid on the nearby Lofoten Islands, finally convinced Hitler that the Allies would open their second front in Norway. He immediately demanded the return of the battle-cruisers *Scharnhorst* and *Gneisenau* and the heavy cruiser *Prinz Eugen* to northern waters. These three warships were in Brest harbour and the subject of constant RAF bombing raids. The German High Command gave orders that the ships were to break out after darkness and attempt a dash up the English Channel to the River Elbe. Escorts would be provided with air cover during daylight. On the night of February 11/12, 1942, RAF Wellington bombers made another raid and shortly afterwards the ships slipped out, escorted by six large destroyers, 34 E-boats and an assortment of flak ships.

The British had been aware that these three dangerous warships might break out and in January 1942 had called a special conference on the matter. It was anticipated the ships might attempt a dash up the English Channel under cover of darkness, to try it in daylight was considered suicidal. The plan therefore decided upon was a night torpedo attack. No individual units were assigned to the task but any conference squadron commander could volunteer himself and his squadron. A diminutive Lt Cdr was the first to reply, offering the services of No 825 Squadron. His offer was accepted although at that stage the authorities knew that his unit was below strength with only six Swordfish and was in the process of working up. It was felt however, that by the time the German ships were ready to break out, 825 would have a full complement of aircraft and crews and be fully trained for the job. The promise of five squadrons of Spitfires as an escort took away any doubts about the raid or Luftwaffe interference if the job had to be done in daylight.

The Lt Cdr was Eugene 'Winkle' Esmonde, DSO, DSC, an Irishman who had joined the RAF way back in 1928 on a short-service commission. As the Air Ministry administered the FAA in those days there was an interchange of air and ground crews with the result that Esmonde spent some of his RAF service aboard aircraft carriers. He then left the RAF and flew with Imperial Airways, predessor of the current British Airways, and he later delivered the first internal air mails in India. In January 1939 the Admiralty offered Esmonde a commission in the FAA, which he accepted and shortly afterwards took command of a Swordfish training squadron. He later commanded No 825 Squadron and from *Victorious* led the first torpedo attack on *Bismarck* in May 1941. The squadron then transferred to the *Ark Royal* but on November 13, 1941, the *Ark* was torpedoed and later sank. The following month Esmonde reformed 825 at Lee-on-Solent with six Swordfish, seven pilots, six observers and six TAGs.

Training got under way and early in February 1942, Esmonde took the squadron to RAF Manston in Kent where the final training was to be done, and to be near the Channel for the strike. On February 11, Esmonde attended the investiture at Buckingham Palace for his DSO, awarded for the *Bismarck* action. Shortly after noon the next day, 825 were alerted. The German ships had broken out, were passing through the Straits of Dover and about 10 miles north east of Calais. Esmonde, still with only six Swordfish, elected to go, although he had been informed that his fighter escort would be late. With his observer, Lt W. H. Williams and TAG Leading Airman W. J. Clinton, he took off in Swordfish W.5984 at 1215. The six aircraft were to attack in two waves of three, Esmonde leading the first with Sub Lt B. Rose with observer Sub Lt E. Lee and TAG Leading Airman Johnson in W.5983, and Sub Lt C. Kingsmill with observer Sub Lt R. M. Samples and TAG Leading Airman D. A. Bunce in W.5907. The second wave was to be led by Lt Thompson in W.4523 with observer Sub Lt Parkinson and TAG Leading Airman E. Topping, followed by Sub Lt Wood in W.5985 with observer Sub Lt Fuller-Wright and TAG Leading Airman Wheeler, finally Sub Lt P. Bligh with observer Sub Lt W. Beynon and TAG Leading Airman Smith brought up the rear in W.5978. Orbiting over the coast, Esmonde waited for his fighter escort. A few minutes later Spitfires arrived out of the murk but instead of the five squadrons promised there were only ten aircraft from No 72 Squadron. The rest, caught off duty, were being rounded up but would be late. Esmonde decided to go and hope that the rest of the Spitfires would catch up. When the Spitfires did turn up the Luftwaffe engaged them to the south of the main action and they had no chance of giving cover to the Swordfish. After 20 minutes flying the Swordfish sighted the enemy. As far as the eye could see there were enemy ships, the guns already twinkling at them. Despite the low cloud base and poor visibility the sky seemed full of Luftwaffe fighters. Protected by inner and outer screens of ships the targets, *Prinz Eugen* leading, followed by *Scharnhorst* and *Gneisenau* looked almost impregnable. Flying at 50 feet the slow biplanes passed over the outer destroyer screen to be met by intense anti-aircraft fire. Esmonde's Swordfish was hit almost immediately causing him to fly erratically. Bf.109s appeared and made firing passes down the formation but the slow speed of the biplanes confused them and they had difficulty lining up. They were joined by FW.190s and at least one fighter went into the sea when the pilot lost control trying to stay with the Swordfish. Tracer bullets set fire to the fabric of Esmonde's aircraft but his gunner Clinton, crawled out of the rear cockpit and sitting astride the fuselage beat the flames out with his gloved hands before returning to his gun. By now Esmonde's aircraft was over the inner screen and there were wide holes through the fabric where heavy shells had hit and gone through. The big ships were putting a heavy barrage of shell fire slightly ahead of him in an effort to bring him down with a wall of water. It was one of these shells, sent to make a watersplash, that ricocheted off the water and took the complete lower port wing off. The Swordfish dipped toward the sea but Esmonde managed to regain control and brought the nose up again. A few seconds later the cockpits were lashed by tracer killing Williams and the gallant Clinton. Wounded in the back and head and more dead than alive Esmonde lined up on the *Scharnhorst* and released his torpedo. More fighters pounced, spraying the Swordfish with gunfire causing it to crash into the sea. Rose, following his leader over the outer screen had been subject to similar attacks. His gunner was killed by the fighters but Lee stood in the rear cockpit, fully exposed to the enemy fire while he shouted warnings to his pilot. A cannon shell passed between Lee and the fuselage to explode against the pilot's armoured backrest. Although wounded Rose managed to regain control only to receive a hit in the main fuel tank. The engine faded but Rose switched to the 15 gallon emergency tank and the Swordfish skimmed the sea as the engine picked up. Streaming petrol Rose lined up and fired his torpedo at the *Prinz Eugen*. With his torpedo gone Rose no longer presented a threat to the enemy and they switched their attacks to the remaining aircraft. Rose managed to clear the inner screen and crash landed into the sea. The last Swordfish of the first wave, Kingsmill, had dropped astern and taken tremendous punishment. With all three crew wounded the Swordfish limped over the inner screen. Fighters pounced again and the two top cylinders of the engine were shot away. It burst into flames and the port wing caught fire. Kingsmill lined up on the *Prinz Eugen* and released his torpedo. Turning south he managed to keep the Swordfish airborne until he cleared the last E-boat before dropping into the sea.

It was now the turn of the second wave. Led by Lt Thompson the three Swordfish, instead of going in line astern like the first wave, flew together as a vic of three. This was undoubtedly done to concentrate the fire power from the rear gunners and hope that the centre aircraft might make a strike at the expense of the other two. Whatever the cause, the three Swordfish crossed the inner screen in ribbons, all the crews wounded. Fighters with flaps and undercarts down to reduce speed still fired at them as a massive waterspout barrage was put up. None of the Swordfish or their crews were ever seen again.

The guns stopped firing and the Germans looked around for the next attack. It had all been in vain, no torpedo had struck home. There were only five survivors, Rose, Lee, Kingsmill, Samples and Bunce. The four officers were awarded the DSO. Leading Airman Bunce, the CGM. For the gallant crews who gave their lives, the only posthumous honour possible, a Mention In Despatches. To the leader, Lt Cdr E. Esmonde, DSO, DSC, went the highest award, the Victoria Cross.

A picture of Lt Cdr E. Esmonde (second on the left) taken when Vice Admiral Sir James Somerville visited *Ark Royal* to congratulate those involved in the *Bismarck* sinking. Esmonde led the first strike from *Victorious* with Swordfish of No 825 Squadron./*IWM*

Whoops....

Above left: Tangled wreckage after L. 2852 crashed into another Swordfish on the night of February 19, 1944 while practising night ADDLs./*via R. C. Jones*

Left: Two Swordfish on MAC-ship *Empire Mackay* after a gale at sea in 1944. Weather was the worst enemy for the smaller carriers./*via R. C. Jones*

Top right: Swordfish L.2761 of No 823 Squadron comes to grief. The squadron was in *Furious* and the fuselage band is red./*via R. C. Jones*

Centre right: This picture shows how when an ATA pilot flew into the Manchester balloon barrage the cable cut through the wing. The Swordfish is L.9726 which was reconditioned by the Fairey Stockport factory in November 1942./*D. Menzies*

Bottom right: A view of the tailplane of L.9726 with balloon cable wrapped around it.

Above left: Swordfish NF.149 seen here on *Macmahon* June 15, 1944. It landed heavily, caught the first wire, sheared both oleos, slid into the second wire and slewed round to finish up on the deck edge. The batsman had about two seconds to jump clear into the safety net. NF.149 is seen here being stripped of equipment prior to being dumped overboard./*J. T. Canham*

Above: One Stringbag tries to eat another in this scene on *Eagle* after a night deck landing in the Clyde 1942. The aircraft forward is from No 813 Squadron and the other from No 824.

Left: B.1 is LS.217 of No.836 Squadron aboard MAC-ship *Macmahon* seen here on May 10, 1944 after bouncing over the first three wires, catching the fourth off centre and hitting the bridge./*J. T. Canham*

Below: Swordfish K.5942 of No.823 Squadron comes to grief. Note the mixed service groundcrew, although the military origin of the two characters on the right seems doubtful./*via R. C. Jones*

Top right: G3 a Swordfish of G Flight of No 836 Squadron shears its undercarriage during a landing on *Macmahon* in 1944.

Bottom right: Swordfish 973 goes over the bow of *Glorious* sometime in 1937. The Swordfish K.59?? was from No 823 Squadron, the band around the fuselage being yellow with black numerals./*via R. C. Jones*

On test

Above: An air-to-air of the enclosed cockpit canopy test Swordfish HS.553. They were known unofficially as Mk.IVs but are now referrred to as MkIIs./*Canadian Armed Forces*

Centre left: Swordfish NR.995/G careers down the runway for a trial RATO (Rocket assisted take-off). The /G after the serial means that regulations required a guard to stand watch over the aircraft as the installation was secret./*IWM*

Bottom left: LS. 295, the test Swordfish for the rocket projectile layout seen here in the Fairey hangar. In the background is Swordfish L.2717 and one of the prototype Albacores./*Fairey Aviation*

Top right: Another view of NR.995/G shortly after lift off. The RATO gear was jettisoned after use. Rockets were particularly useful for heavily laden Swordfish taking off the short decks of MAC-ships./*IWM*

Centre right: A Swordfish on the floating airstrip *Lily*. Flown by Ray Jeffs the Swordfish has just landed on the strip at Lamlash and the sagging is apparent under the wheels. The strip was 526 feet long and 60 feet wide, the Swordfish weighed 9,000lb. The brainchild of Petty Officer R. M. Hamilton, *Lily* consisted of hundreds of hexagonal buoyancy cans with a flat surface laid on top. It was to be capable of easy dismantling, transport and assembly./*IWM*

Bottom right: An early composite Swordfish III is V.4689/G seen here at Boscombe Down for ASV trials. A small radome is also mounted under the inner starboard wing./*IWM*

Stringbag ops

The following sequence of events is in no way meant to be definitive but to be read for pleasure or as a guide to more serious reading and research.

1939

One of the earliest attacks carried out by Swordfish was September 14 when a formation attacked U.30 as it was trying to torpedo the SS *Fanad Head*. This ship had already been torpedoed by U.39, itself sunk by Skua aircraft from *Ark Royal*.

1940

During the Norwegian campaign Swordfish were active as the only support strike aircraft for the land forces. Nos. 816 and 818 Squadrons embarked in *Furious* carried out the first large scale FAA torpedo attack on April 11 when they tried to sink two German destroyers in Trondheim. Unfortunately the torpedoes grounded in shallow water. Relieved by *Ark Royal* and *Glorious* the *Furious* was used for ferrying RAF aircraft. Flying from *Ark Royal* Swordfish bombed Vaernes aerodrome, squadrons 810 and 820 attacking in daylight from 6 000 feet. On May 9, six Swordfish attacked the railway line east of Narvik. Taking two hours to fly there because of high winds the strike force split up, one section going to bomb the Nordalshoen viaduct near the Swedish border, and the others overturning a train in Hunddallen

railway station. At least five Swordfish were lost in action during this period. The *Glorious*, loaded with RAF and FAA aircraft from the withdrawal from Norway was intercepted by the *Gneisenau* and *Scharnhorst* and sunk. The latter was hit by a torpedo from the destroyer *Acasta* as it too was sunk. *Scharnhorst* set off for Trondheim to effect repairs and was dive-bombed by Skua's, unsuccessfully. On June 21 six Swordfish at Hatston in the Orkneys were alerted to make a strike on her. Three from No 821 and three from another squadron were hastily fitted with long range tanks in the rear cockpit and loaded with a torpedo. Led by Lt V. A. T. Smith, RAN, the observer in Swordfish P.4144 and piloted by Sub Lt J. H. Stenning the six aircraft took off. Climbing to 8 000 feet they found the *Scharnhorst* off the Norwegian coast and dived through considerable flak in an effort to get inside the destroyer screen, but all the torpedoes missed and two Swordfish were shot down.

On June 23 *Ark Royal* arrived at Gibraltar with three Swordfish squadrons, Nos 810, 818 and 820 embarked. She was to join a task force, known as Force H, sent to invite the French Fleet either to join the Allies or suffer the consequences. The French Fleet consisted of two new battle-cruiser the *Strasbourg*, and *Dunkerque*, two battleships, several light cruisers, some destroyers and submarines, all at Oran or Mers-el-Kebir on the Moroccan coast. With the collapse of France and the entry of Italy into the war the British were concerned about their eventual use, particularly as the French themselves were split into two factions, the Vichy and Free French. The Fleet declined to join the British or be interned. At 1753 on July 3, Force H opened fire, Swordfish from *Ark Royal* spotting for the guns. Five other Swordfish dropped mines in the entrance to Mers-el-Kebir harbour. The *Strasbourg* broke out with a destroyer escort and made off to the east. Six Swordfish set off in pursuit, their bombs

Left: Rare picture of a Swordfish immediately after being catapulted off the deck of *Ark Royal* in the South Atlantic during the *Graf Spee* episode in 1939.

Top: A recently re-sprayed Swordfish V.4697 at Fayid, Egypt on November 16, 1942. Note the filter under the cowling and the black undersurfaces for night operations. This aircraft had previously been with No810 Squadron on *Illustrious* and took part in the raid on Diego Suarez./*Howard Levy*

Above: A Swordfish G of an unknown unit gets airborne with two depth charges./*via D. Birch*

straddling her but scoring no hits. A second strike was sent out at 2000 with torpedoes but they all missed. This was the first time that Swordfish from *Ark Royal* had attacked a capital ship at sea with torpedoes. Reconnaissance the next day revealed the the *Dunkerque*, although grounded, was not out of action. The two squadrons of Swordfish made an attack in line astern, diving with their torpedoes from 7 000 feet and scoring six hits. While this was going on the *Hermes* had been shadowing the newly commissioned French battleship, the *Richelieu*. On July 8 six Swordfish of No 814 Squadron from *Hermes* attacked her with torpedoes. The attack had to be made between two rows of merchant ships and one hit was obtained damaging the *Richelieu's* propeller shafts, steering gear and causing flooding aft. She was out of action for over a year.

July 8 was a busy day for the FAA as apart from these actions, Nos 813 and 824 Squadrons embarked in *Eagle* were involved in two inconclusive actions with the Italian Fleet off Calabria. On July 10, No 813 made a dusk torpedo attack in Augusta harbour in Sicily. Hits were made on a destroyer and tanker. No 824, now ashore in Egypt, had a good month by sinking two destroyers, three submarines and a depot ship for the expenditure of nine torpedoes. Later in the month their Swordfish made attacks on Tobruk.

After the distasteful action at Oran, Force H moved into the Mediterranean where, on August 2 nine Swordfish from *Ark Royal* flew off to attack Cagliari on Sardinia with three others carrying mines for the harbour. Led by Lt Cdr G. B. Hodgkinson the Swordfish bombed hangars and buildings at Elmos airfield. Four hangars were wrecked, buildings set on fire and four aircraft on the ground destroyed. One Swordfish was lost, Lt R. N. Everett the leader of the mine laying flight was hit in the engine and made a forced landing on Elmos while the battle was raging. He and his crew were made POW. The returning Swordfish had a 150 mile trip back to the carrier and after being in the air for over four hours three of them landed with only five gallons of petrol left in their tanks.

Early in August the Swordfish from *Eagle* spotted for the bombardment of Bardia and then went ashore when *Eagle* went into Alexandria harbour. With Nos 813 and 824 squadrons ashore, Air Commodore R. Collishaw, Air Officer Commanding the Western Desert, applied for some torpedo carrying aircraft to help deal with enemy shipping off the Libyan coast. Three Swordfish from No 813 squadron were detached and for the first few nights carried out anti-submarine patrols. On August 21 an RAF Blenheim on dusk patrol spotted a submarine depot ship lying in Bomba Bay with a submarine heading in from seaward. Early next morning the senior officer of the squadron, Captain Patch, RM, arrived to take command and flew the flight to Sidi Barrani. Armed with torpedoes they took off and headed out to sea in V formation. Flying low the Swordfish routed themselves 50 miles from the coast to avoid any prowling Italian fighters. Turning in towards the coast they found themselves running straight for Bomba Bay. When still four miles out they could see a submarine dead ahead on the surface moving at slow speed, and beyond at the entrance to An-el-Gazala creek were other vessels. Th submarine opened fire on them as they went down to 30 feet. Captain Patch, with Midshipman C. J. Woodley as his observer faked a pass to starboard, then to port, before dropping his torpedo at 300 yards. It hit the submarine amidships causing it to blow up in a spectacular explosion. Captain Patch then turned out to sea. The port Swordfish of the three, flown by Lt J. W. G. Wellham with Petty Officer A. H. Marsh as his observer flew on towards the other ships, now identified as the submarine depot ship, a destroyer and a submarine. The last Swordfish flown by Lt N. A. F. Cheesman with Sub Lt F. Stovin-Bradford as observer flew to within 350 yards of the shore to make his attack from landward. Lt Cheesman's torpedo hit the submarine a few seconds before Lt Wellham's hit the depot ship below the bridge. Turning to seaward the Swordfish crews heard a terrific explosion and looking back saw the three ships disappearing from sight in a cloud of steam and smoke. All the Swordfish returned safely, only one sustaining a hit. The three old Stringbags had in fact sunk all four enemy ships with three torpedoes in a matter of minutes! Captain Patch was awarded the DSO and the rest of the crews were also decorated. The squadrons re-joined *Eagle* and on September 1 the Fleet had a welcome addition in the form of *Illustrious* with Nos 815 and 819 Squadrons with Swordfish and No 806 with Fulmars. Early in September the Swordfish from *Eagle* made a strike on Rhodes but lost four aircraft to Italian Fiat CR.42 fighter biplanes. From then on the four squadrons of Swordfish made their presence felt by dive bombing airfields, mining harbours and wreaked havoc with Italian shipping.

During September/October, Nos 816 and 825 Squadrons in *Furious* with the Home Fleet attacked Trondheim and Tromso in Norway. The latter action being the first squadron-sized torpedo attack to be carried out at night, a month before Taranto. Back in the Med, Swordfish from *Ark Royal* on September 2/3 made two strikes on Cagliari led by Lt Cdr M. Johnstone and after the Carrier's refit they went again on November 9. On September 17, 15 Swordfish from *Illustrious* attacked vessels in Benghazi harbour sinking two Italian destroyers and damaging other ships. There was little action during October as plans for Taranto were in train concluding with the famous raid which is described elsewhere. On the morning of November 27, Force H was escor-

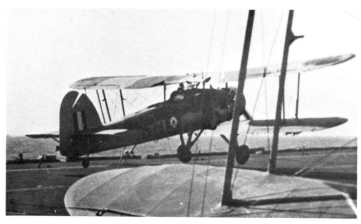

Top left: Swordfish P.4206 5G of No 824 Squadron being flown here by Sub Lt P. G. Lawrence out from Alexandria./*Cdr S. H. Suthers*

Centre left: The packed flight deck of *Eagle* off Mombasa in April 1941. The Swordfish are from Nos 813 and 824 Squadrons which carried out anti-submarine patrols and searches. On the June 6, 1941 Swordfish E5B found the *Elbe* and sank her./*Cdr S. H. Suthers*

Above left: Sub Lt S. H. Suthers of No 824 Squadron at the moment of touch down in 5H on the *Eagle* flight deck. Sub Lt Suthers flying 5C sank a destroyer of an Italian force off Port Sudan on April 3, 1941./*Cdr S. H. Suthers*

ting an east bound convoy and were in process of handing over to the new escorts when a Swordfish out on patrol reported the Italian Fleet south of Sardinia. It consisted of two battle ships, six cruisers and 16 destroyers. Another Swordfish was sent out to relieve the first and keep track of the Italians. In an effort to slow them down and bring them to battle, 11 Swordfish were flown off at 1100. Led by Lt Cdr M. Johnstone the strike aircraft, all with torpedoes, reached the Italian Fleet after 20 minutes flying. Div-

Above: Swordfish 5C of No. 821 Squadron in a pleasing study as the pilot joins the circuit for *Ark Royal./Cdr R. N. Everett*

Above left: Fine shot of Swordfish 5C of No 821 Squadron breaking over the bows of *Ark Royal.* The arrestor hook is already down./*Cdr R. N. Everett*

ing out of the sun the Swordfish went after the battleships, dropping their torpedoes from a range of 700 yards. The *Vittorio Veneto* was seen to be hit abaft the after funnel and other explosions were seen astern of her and in front of the first cruiser. An hour later nine Swordfish went off on another strike, this time led by Lt Cdr J. A. Stewart-Moore. In the face of intense flak the Swordfish dived down but as they released their torpedoes the cruisers turned away although it was thought one had been hit. To close 1940 the Swordfish from *Illustrious* attacked airfields in the Aegean and Dodecanese and in December bombed Rhodes and a convoy off Sfax. Two large Italian merchant ships were torpedoed and sunk by six Swordfish in a night attack.

1941

On February 2, eight Swordfish from *Ark Royal* went to attack the Tirso dam in Sardinia. Flying through strong gusty winds with icing conditions one Swordfish got separated and returned to the Ark. Two had to jettison their torpedoes because of heavy icing and one was shot down. The other four released their torpedoes against the dam but apparently had no effect. The Azienda oil refinery was the next target. A strike force of 14 Swordfish left *Ark Royal* early in the morning and 11 of these made the attack with 250lb bombs, again with no effective results. Four other Swordfish had been despatched to mine the entrance to La Spezia harbour and three more to spot for the Fleet's bombardment of Genoa. The only aircraft lost was a Swordfish that flew into a balloon cable.

Six Swordfish of No 815 Squadron arrived in Greece on March 11 and proceeded to Paramythia for operations against Valona and Durazzo harbours. Despite shallow waters and night fighters seven sorties were flown against Durazzo and 12 against Valona resulting in five torpedo hits and two probable hits on shipping. The CO was unfortunately lost on the first sortie.

When Greece was overrun the surviving Swordfish moved to Maleme on Crete. Here Lt F. M. A. Torrens-Spence took over as CO and continued to operate until April when they withdrew with two Swordfish. RAF reconnaissance reported a force of Italian ships 100 miles east of Cape Passero in Sicily heading eastwards.

On March 28, *Formidable*, sent to fill the gap after *Illustrious* was bombed and withdrawn for repairs, launched a spotting force of four Albacores and one Swordfish to search for it. The convoy was located in poor visibility south-west of Crete. Advancing to meet them were the Light Forces under Vice-Admiral H. D. Pridham-Wippell, KCB, CVO. *Formidable* ranged 10 Albacores, four Swordfish and 13 Fulmars but at 1000 only launched six Albacores under Lt Cdr W. H. G. Saunt, DSC, with two Fulmars as fighter escort. Arriving on the scene they found the old enemy *Vittorio Veneto* engaging Pridham-Wippell's Light Force. The Albacores attacked in two sub-flights of three and managed to get one hit on the port quarter. Meanwhile, three Swordfish of No 815 squadron based at Maleme were led by Lt Torrens-Spence to attack the cruisers. Sighting the enemy at noon they attacked the rear cruiser but observed no results. A second strike from *Formidable* consisting of three Albacores, two Swordfish and two Fulmars took off just as the first strike returned. Led by Lt Cdr J. Dalyell-Stead the second strike sighted the *Vittorio Veneto* south of Cape Matapan screened by two destroyers on each bow. The big ship took avoiding action but the five biplanes all appeared to make hits. Unfortunately the strike leader was lost in this action. Although not mortally hit, the Italian battleship continued slowly westward and was seen by a shadowing Albacore. A Swordfish floatplane was despatched fom the flagship, HMS *Orion* to join the relieving Albacore and the two kept watch until dusk. It was decided to send in one more strike so six Albacores and two Swordfish were flown off led by Lt Cdr Saunt. The enemy fleet was found to be sailing in five columns with the *Vittorio Veneto* in the centre. The strike force was greeted by a tremedous barrage of gunfire causing them to turn away to starboard and attack independently from different angles. In the ensuring confusion most

Above left: Swordfish HS.164 2F of No 810 Squadron flying over the sea off Tanga in November 1942. Nos 810 and 829 both took part in the Diego Suarez operation and were then shore-based at Tanga and Port Reitz until early 1943 when *Illustrious* returned to the UK./*Cdr R. N. Everett*

Centre left: Photographs of Swordfish on the catapult are rare but here is a good one of 5C of No 821 Squadron on the starboard catapult of *Ark Royal* complete with bombs. Catapults were originated by the Royal Aircraft Establishment at Farnborough in 1922. In 1937 the RAE began work on an Admiralty requirement for a catapult would be capable of launching aircraft at the rate of one every 40 seconds. This was tested on *Illustrious* in May 1940 and the new trolley mechanism was designed to be adjusted for all FAA aircraft; earlier ones could only take certain types of aircraft. In October 1942 a simplified form of accelerator with twin tracks was tried and used operationally for the first time in the Battle of Cape Matapan. As a result all the new Fleet carriers were fitted with the new system./*Cdr R. N. Everett*

Bottom left: Swordfish just about to catch the wire on *Argus.* 2C is probably from No 812 Squadron, embarked in *Argus* for ferry operations in the Mediterranean in 1941./*IWM*

Top right: Swordfish of No 810 Squadron fly ashore to Jamaica on October 1, 1941 after being on the Atlantic run with *Furious.* 2C appears to be V.4444./*via R. C. Jones*

of the strike force believed they had dropped at the battleship. The Swordfish from Maleme also made a second strike, attacking to the rear of the force. Either one of these Swordfish or one of the attacking force hit the cruiser *Pola* stopping her engines and electric power. The cruisers *Zara* and *Fiume* were detached to assist *Pola* and all three were sunk in the night action that followed.

Eagle was in Alexandria with her aircraft ashore when an RAF report came in from Aden to say a destroyer flotilla of the Italian Navy had left Massawa on April 2, heading north. Commander C. L. Keighly-Peach led 17 Swordfish from Nos 813 and 824 Squadrons from Alexandria to Port Sudan, covering the 1 200 miles in two days. Eight Swordfish were sent out independently to search for the enemy ships while the rest were kept bombed up at readiness. Commander Keighly-Peach made a search himself off Port Sudan and about 10 miles out he saw a Swordfish diving towards the sea. Going to investigate he found the Italian destroyers and attacked one himself. Just missing, he raced back to Port Sudan and alerted the main force. From then on Swordfish shadowed the destroyers and attacked in relays as fast as they could re-fuel and re-arm. Sub Lt S. H. Suthers dropped two bombs between the funnels of one ship while Midshipman E. Sergeant scored six hits with one stick of bombs. The crew abandoned the first ship and it sank an hour later, the second one disappearing in 30 seconds. Two other destroyers were found beached and abandoned while the fifth had turned back to Massawa but scuttled herself in the harbour just before the British troops arrived.

By the end of April German-inspired activities provoked a rebellion in Iraq. *Hermes* was recalled from the Indian Ocean to patrol the Persian Gulf. Six Swordfish of No 814 Squadron made a demonstration flight over Basra on May 3 and on the 7th, because of the distance of the carrier from the scene of the action, a small strike force was based ashore at Shaibah. Between May 4th and 16th ten dive-bombing attacks were made on railway bridges, petrol and oil tanks, barracks and troops concentrations. Due to the accurate fire of the Iraqi irregulars, one Swordfish had to force land near barracks at Samawa. The Iraqis advanced,

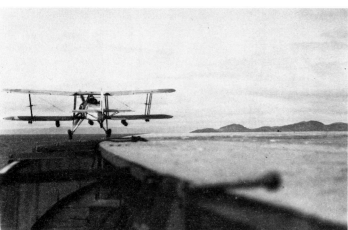

opening fire as they did so. Lt J. H. Dundas, the leader of the strike, saw this and coming down he made a difficult landing. Taking on board the stranded crew he succeeded in taking off in spite of a double load, the appalling ground surface and heavy small arms fire.

On May 22, 1941 after a difficult reconnaissance, a FAA Maryland of No 771 Squadron confirmed that the *Bismarck* was at sea. With in hours the Home Fleet had put to sea also, accompanied by the carrier *Victorious*. Her small complement of aircraft consisted of No 825 Squadron who embarked with only 48 hours notice and with only nine Swordfish. Six Fulmers of No 800 Squadron made up the rest. *Bismarck* was shadowed until the night of May 24/25 when Lt Cdr E. Esmonde led the nine Swordfish in a strike against her. One hit was obtained on her armoured belt but this was a considerable achievement on a fast-moving target at night. Contact with the German ship was then lost until May 26. *Ark Royal* had been alerted and moved up from Gibraltar taking·off for a strike that afternoon. In poor visibility and low cloud the strike force of 15 Swordfish attacked HMS *Sheffield* by mistake. Fortunately she evaded all the torpedoes although some exploded prematurely. A second strike led by Lt Cdr P. G. T. Coode and consisting of 15 Swordfish attacked again individually. Two hits were obtained one destroying the steering gear and jamming the rudders. Reduced to steaming an unknown track she was hounded all night and finally sunk the following morning by the big guns of the Home Fleet and Force H. A third strike of Swordfish was airborne when this happened and they jettisoned their torpedoes to land back on *Ark Royal*.

On the night of June 16 five Swordfish armed with torpedoes were sent to intercept a Vichy French destroyer, the *Chevalier Paul*, which was known to be rushing reinforcements to Syria from Salonika to take part in the Syrian Campaign. One Swordfish discovered the destroyer moving north of Cyprus at high speed and went in to the attack. It was joined by two of the others and a hit was made in the boiler room bringing the destroyer to a stop. One Swordfish failed to return. Three went out the following morning to look for the damaged ship but found only empty boats, wreckage and an empty Swordfish dinghy. The *Chevalier Paul* had sunk soon after being hit but two other French destroyers went to her aid and also picked up the ditched Swordfish crew.

With the German attack on Russia in June the FAA received additional tasks in the way of support for the new ally both by direct and indirect means. When the minelayer *Adventurer* delivered a large number of mines to Archangel it was decided to strike at enemy lines of communication in northern Norway. *Victorious* and *Furious* were despatched with two cruisers and six destroyers to attack Kirkenes and Petsamo. The strike was launched on the afternoon of July 30. *Victorious* sent 20 Albacores and nine Fulmars against Kirkenes and *Furious* sent nine Albacores, nine Swordfish of No 812 Squadron and six Fulmars to Petsamo. An enemy shadower reported the force but it was decided to carry on. The German defences were alerted at Kirkenes and the force lost 11 Albacores and two Fulmars for two Bf. 110s and one Bf.109 plus a Ju.87 shot down by the only undamaged Albacore out of the 20. At Petsamo one Albacore was lost and two Fulmars.

No 812 Squadron had been part of Force H and after spending some time aboard *Ark Royal* and *Argus* found themselves at Gibraltar. Now fitted with ASV their Swordfish operated at night in the Straits and between November 30 and December 21 flew 300 hours on this duty. In three weeks no less than five U-boats were damaged, the ASV proving its worth. On the night of December 21/22, U.451 was sunk by one of the squadron's Swordfish, the first submarine to be sunk at night by an aircraft.

1942

February 12 saw the classic attack by six Swordfish of No 825 Squadron on the three German capital ships as they dashed up the Channel.

In late 1941 there had been some concern that the Vichy French on Madagascar (now the Malagasy Republic) would allow the Japanese use of the bases there and thus cut off the Allied supply route round the Cape to the Middle East. An amphibious assault was launched spearheaded by the *Illustrious* with Nos 810 and 829 Squadrons with Swordfish and the *Indomitable*. Called Operation Ironclad, the objective was the occupation of Diego Suarez. On May 5 a strike force of Albacores from *Indomitable* bombed the airfield and set the hangar on fire. The *Illustrious* flew off three strike forces of six Swordfish, the first armed with torpedoes attacked a French sloop, the *D'Entrecasteaux*, without results, and then torpedoed the armed merchant cruiser *Bougainville* which blew up. The second force, armed with depth charges sank the submarine *Bevezieres*. The third, armed with bombs, dropped leaflets and an ultimatum to the Governor before bombing a gun battery and the sloop *D'Entrecasteaux*. The leader of this force, flown by Lt R. N. Everett and the CO of No 810 Squadron, was hit in the engine by anti-aircraft fire and had to ditch in the sea near the beach. Taken prisoner, Everett and his crew were released after the occupation of Antsirane. Later the same morning the French sloop was again bombed by Swordfish as it tried to get under way, and was beached. Three more Swordfish then bombed it just to make sure. Next day, May 6, a Swordfish spotted for the bombardment of gun emplacements by the destroyer *Laforey* and another piloted by

Top left: K.8422 4H believed to be of No 820 Squadron. Note the wavy camouflage line./*Fleet Air Arm Museum*

Centre left: A Swordfish leaves the flight deck for an early morning sortie.

Bottom left: Swordfish K.8418 5K of No 824 Squadron gets in close during the work up period at Alexandria in 1941./*Cdr S. H. Suthers*

Top: Swordfish floatplane V.4367 being lowered over the side of HMS *Malaya* with the engine already running and the crew aboard./*IWM*

Above: Observer's view of Stringbags setting off on a patrol./*via R. C. Jones*

Sub Lt F. H. Alexander, sank the submarine *La Heros* with depth charges. Three other Swordfish dropped dummy paratroops to the south-west to draw off Vichy forces. Six enemy aircraft were shot down and resistance ended early on the 7th. During the six months that followed before the end of French resistance all over the island, the naval air squadrons were used mainly for reconnaissance but took part in the final assault on positions in September.

This was the last action the Swordfish fought while operating from the Fleet carriers. Thereafter they was replaced by Albacores, Barracudas and Avengers. This great biplane then went on to a new career operating from escort carriers and MAC-ships.

Training trends

Far left: A dual Swordfish being launched off the catapult at Gosport in 1939. It was still in use in 1941./*Fox Photos*

Top left: Unusual is this late dual conversion HS.228 taken at an unknown airfield. In the background a FAA communications Proctor is taking off./*IWM*

Centre left, above: K.8871 J out on a training sortie off the coast of Scotland. This aircraft was delivered to the FAA on April 29, 1937 but is seen here in service with No 785 Training squadron at Crail./*Aeroplane*

Centre left, below: Swordfish could be stored in large number due to its folding wing arrangement. In this picture there are seven parked in a hangar./*via R. C. Jones*

Below: Loading torpedoes for training TSR pilots at a RNAS. The nearest aircraft is L.9715 which in 1940 belonged to C Flight of Y Squadron at the TTU Abbotsinch, where this photo was probably taken./*IWM*

Above: A formation of training Swordfish of No 785 Squadron based at Crail. Nearest aircraft is L.2728 K which was delivered to Gosport on June 28, 1937./*IWM*

Above right: Swordfish of No.1 Naval Air Gunners' School at Yarmouth, Nova Scotia, Canada in 1944. Operating under the RCAF this unit trained TAGs for squadrons working up in America with Lend-Lease aircraft./*Public Archives of Canada*

Right: A batsman brings a Swordfish in on *Smiter* April 1945. Batsmen led a dangerous life on carriers frequently needing the backup net./*via R. C. Jones*

Below: Three very colourful Swordfish IIs wearing invasion stripes out on a training flight. They were to be used for patrolling the Channel on D-Day and after./*IWM*

Far right, top: Swordfish M2.C at the moment of catching the wire as it lands aboard *Argus*./*IWM*

Far right, bottom: A wet start to a day's flying. Swordfish taxying in a high wind. Note the matelots on the wingtips of each aircraft, the nearest one being V.4438 B./*IWM*

Escort carriers and MAC–ships

Escort Carriers

When Europe fell to the Germans during the summer of 1940, Britain found herself isolated and started the ship convoy system to survive. At the outbreak of war Germany had 57 operational U-boats, by the end of 1942 she had 485 of which 68 were Italian. By this time U-boats were being built faster than the Allies could destroy them. During the period 1939-45 some 75 000 merchant ships were escorted in British controlled convoys with a loss of 574 or one in every 131 that sailed on Atlantic crossings alone. In fact U-boats accounted for 2 775 merchant ships during World War II, or a rate of 40 a month. Against this, no fewer than 781 German and 85 Italian submarines were sunk.

The limited radius of action of RAF Coastal Command aircraft early in the war operating from Britain, Iceland and later, North America, left a large 'gap' in the central Atlantic and it was here that the U-boats scored most of their successes. Long range Focke Wulf Fw.200 Condors shadowed convoys and relayed information to the U-boats who operated in packs. An early effort to stop the Condors involved the use of Fighter Catapult Ships where a Fulmar or Hurricane were embarked on a converted merchant ship. When the shadower appeared the fighter was catapulted off to intercept it. Five such ships were converted initially and ten launches were made resulting in the destruction of one Fw.200 and another damaged. Each launch however meant that the shadower was driven off and the effect was enough for the Admiralty to order 35 more Catapult Armed Merchant ships. From May 1941 to August 1943 the CAM ships made 170 round voyages with eight operational launches being made for the destruction of six enemy aircraft and damage to three others.

The appalling losses in the Atlantic and the success of the CAM ships resulted in the Admiralty resurrecting a pre-war idea of using auxiliary aircraft carriers, later to be known as escort carriers. Ironically it was a captured German ship, the *Hannover* that was first converted and re-named *Audacity*. The existing hull was fitted with 460 foot flush deck with two arrestor wires and a crash barrier. Armed with sturdy Grumman Martlet fighters of No 802 Squadron, *Audacity* made two round voyages on the Gibralter run before she was torpedoed and sunk on December 21, 1941. In that time her Martlets had shot down five Fw.200, damaged three more and drove off another. The fighters also flew anti-submarine patrols and this resulted in them sharing the destruction of U.131 with the escorting destroyers. The short career of *Audacity* had proved the effectiveness of escort carriers and one year later seven were in commission; the British-built *Activity* and the American-built *Archer, Attacker, Avenger, Biter, Battler* and *Dasher*. The Royal Navy relied more on the American-built escort carriers (known as CVEs) which allowed British shipyards to concentrate on frigates, corvettes etc. Only 24 ships were lost to enemy action in the 27 convoys that escort carriers accompanied. Apart from *Avenger* making one convoy to Russia in September 1942, the American escort carriers did not begin trade protection convoys in the Atlantic until late April

1943. The causes of delay were numerous. The first was the need to support the North African Landings. Then extensive modifications were required by the Admiralty after *Dasher* blew up and *Avenger* sank after being hit with only one torpedo. Frequent re-fits were necessary because the hull and propulsion systems had not been designed for the rigours of wartime use.

Avenger joined convoy PQ.18 off Iceland on September 9 1942, after embarking three Swordfish and 12 Sea Hurricanes. On an anti-submarine patrol one of the Swordfish reported a U-boat and shortly afterwards U.589 was sunk by escorting destroyers. The invasion of North Africa, which occurred in November 1942, required the escort carriers and none were available for convoy escort duties until February 1943 when *Dasher* embarked six Swordfish of No 816 Squadron and nine Sea Hurricanes of No 891 for Convoy JW.53, (JW meant eastbound, RA westbound), only to return two days later with weather damage. *Biter* was the first escort carrier on the North Atlantic run in April 1943. She went on 16 trans-Atlantic and Gibralter convoys embarking Swordfish and Wildcats of No 811 Squadron on each occasion. Her aircraft shared in the destruction of U.203 with *Pathfinder* and U.89 with *Lagan* and *Broadway*. In the early hours of May 23 1943, U.752 spotted a homeward-bound convoy some 750 miles west of Ireland and started to shadow it. A Swordfish flown by Sub Lt H. Horrocks on an anti-submarine patrol saw the U-boat and under cover of cloud managed to get within 300 yards before firing his rocket projectiles. One of them pierced the hull inflicting considerable damage and U.752, unable to dive, surfaced to fight it out. However, the Swordfish had called up a Martlet fighter which strafed the U-boat's bridge killing the captain and some of the crew. The tanks were flooded and U.752 sank, the first case of an aircraft from an escort carrier being solely responsible for sinking a U-boat and the first time a rocket projectile had been fired operationally by any of the Western Allies. The R/P had a 25lb solid head and fired at a range of 600 yards was capable of penetrating both the near and far plating of a U-boats pressure hull. There were no further FAA successes against U-boats in the Atlantic until Swordfish of No 842 Squadron, embarked in *Fencer* sank U.666 in the Eastern Atlantic in February 1944.

In July 1943 *Unicorn* joined *Illustrious* for a diversionary sweep to draw attention away from the Allied landings in Sicily. Embarked in *Unicorn* were Nos 818 and 824 Squadrons with 13 Swordfish between them and ten Seafires for fighter cover. U-boats were achieving significant results in the Indian Ocean where the loss of *Hermes* left a serious gap in the defences. It was September 1943 before another carrier could be spared to provide escort to convoys. This was *Battler* with 12 Swordfish and six Seafires of No 842 Squadron embarked. In the close escort role

the anti-submarine team had no success so Admiral Somerville adopted the American hunter/killer tactics. Two enemy supply ships were found on March 12, 1944, by one of the Swordfish. It destroyed one and homed nearby ships onto the other.

Chaser was the first escort carrier to complete the round trip to Russia during February/March, 1944. She had embarked, 11 Swordfish and 11 Wildcats of No 816 Squadron. Early in March her aircraft sank two U-boats, U.366 and U.973, and shared in the destruction of U.472 with *Onslaught*. It became standard to have two escort carriers on the Russian convoys and for JW/RA.58 in March/April 1944 these were *Activity* and *Tracker*. *Activity* had No 819 Squadron embarked with three Swordfish and seven Wildcats. This force sank U.288, shared U.355 with *Beagle* and damaged three other U-boats. Six shadowing aircraft were shot down, a not insignificant result. Thereafter until convoy JW/RA.66, Swordfish were embarked in the escort carriers involved with each convoy. These were *Activity, Striker, Fencer, Vindex, Campania* and *Nairana*. The protection afforded to the convoys resulted in the loss of only four merchant ships out of 304 despatched. Seven U-boats alone were sunk in only three convoys, an outstanding action occurred when Swordfish from No 842 Squadron embarked in *Fencer*, sank three in May 1944. The U-boats did not like these odds. Most were fitted with the new schnorkel equipment and limited their operations to coastal waters. The hunter/killer sweep tactics used in the Indian Ocean but mainly by the Americans were tried with the newly commissioned *Vindex*. Flying day and night in terrible weather conditions the Swordfish of No 825 Squadron worked with the 2nd and 6th Escort Groups in the south-west approaches. On March 15 1944, the Swordfish shared the destruction of U.653 and on the second sweep in May shared again when U.765 was sunk.

Top left: Typical weather-deck conditions aboard an escort carrier as on the Russian convoys./*IWM*

Centre left: A Swordfish taking off *Smiter* which was not commissioned until August 1945 and thus saw no action./ *Crown Cropright*

Bottom left: The narrowness of the escort carrier deck is seen in this picture as a Swordfish is batted on./*IWM*

Top: A Swordfish at the moment of taking off, this one coded M is armed with a torpedo./*IWM*

Above: The wreckage aboard the *Empire Mackay* after a gale in 1944. D3 LS.218 has Merchant Navy stencilled near the tail. The other two aircraft are D2 LS.277 and D1 LS.287./*Public Archives of Canada*

During the first strike on *Tirpitz* on April 3, 1944, Swordfish of No 842 Squadron embarked in *Fencer* provided anti-submarine patrols and her Wildcats, Fleet protection. No 842 also provided three Swordfish for similar duties for the second series of strikes but embarked in *Furious*. *Nabob* was torpedoed on August 22, 1944, by U.354 but managed to get back to Scapa Flow. U.354 was sunk three days later by Swordfish from *Vindex*. FAA aircraft flying from Fleet and escort carriers between April 26, 1944 and May 8, 1945, undertook 30 operations off the Norwegian coast. For various strikes in April, May and June, *Striker* embarked No 824 Squadron with 12 Swordfish. October saw *Campania* in action with 12 Swordfish and four Wildcats of No 813 Squadron and for a further strike in January 1945, No 813 had eight Swordfish and eight Wildcats. Also in January, No 835 Squadron had embarked 14 Swordfish and six Wildcats for a strike. An example of one of the strikes concerns No 813 Squadron. Embarked in *Campania* the aircraft were launched on the night of January 28 for a strike on Vaagso. After being illuminated by flares, three trawlers were sunk by rocket projectiles.

Mac-Ships

Although a considerable number of escort carriers was on order, the rate of delivery and urgent need of them elsewhere created a problem in the central Atlantic early in the war. The Admiralty gave the go-ahead for the conversion of two grain carrying ships to operate aircraft and carry cargo. They specified a minimum flight deck length of 490 feet and a speed of 14/15 knots but had to accept 390 feet and 11/12 knots so that standard cargo hulls could be used. The Lend-Lease Vought-Sikorsky Kingfisher had been the original choice of aircraft for the new ships but in the

Above: Swordfish H2 comes in a bit high to land on *Empire Mackay* January 20, 1944 off Halifax, Canada./*Public Archives of Canada*

Centre left: Two Swordfish B3 LS.434 and B4 LS.225 warm up at RNAS Dartmouth Nova Scotia early in 1945./*J. T. Canham*

Bottom left: LS.434 B3 over RCNAS Dartmouth in January 1945 after crossing the Atlantic on MAC-ship *Macmahon.*Note the baker's head insignia./*J. T. Canham*

Top right: LS.225 B4 over the sea early 1945. It was, with B.3, from *Macmahon./J. T. Canham*

Centre right: The cramped flight deck space on a MAC-ship is evident in this picture of *Macmahon* in the summer of 1944. Note the B3 marked on the lower wing root./*J. T. Canham*

Bottom right: A Swordfish leaving MAC-ship *Macmahon* in the summer of 1944. The ship has turned away from the convoy to launch its aircraft./*J. T. Canham*

event the Swordfish was used. It was also planned to have one Martlet fighter but for some reason this did not materialise. The ships were known as Merchant Aircraft Carriers (MAC-ship) and operated three or four Swordfish depending on whether the converted ship was a grain carrier or tanker. The grain MAC-ships had a lift and small hangar but the tankers had no hangar but had a slightly longer flight deck. The Swordfish were pooled from Nos 836, 840 and 860 (Royal Netherlands Navy) Squadrons with a home base at Maydown in Northern Ireland. Some 92 Swordfish were on strength by early 1944, many with Merchant Navy stencilled on the aft fuselage in place of Royal Navy. The procedure to join a MAC-ship was to fly along Lough Foyle east to Rathlin Island and then north-east up the Clyde where the MAC-ship would wait for them to land on.

Ltd. Cdr R. W. Slater became the first pilot to land a Swordfish aboard a MAC-ship when he landed on *Empire Macalpine* in May 1943. It was none too soon. In the four months, August to November 1942 the U-boats sank 2 000 000 tons of shipping, most of it in convoy. The few escort carriers available had been withdrawn for the North African landings. March 1943 saw 97 ships sunk in twenty days. The Naval Staff in alarm declared that if the sinkings continued they would not be able to support the convoy system as an effective means of defence. The first MAC-ship deployed with a convoy was *Empire Macalpine* when in September 1943 ONS.18 and ON.22 combined to have 66 merchant ships and 17 escorts. Flying conditions were bad at first but in the first sortie the Swordfish returned to find the ship in dense fog. Using its own radar in conjunction with the set on the ship it homed in and with help of aldis lamps turned on to assist along with a streamed fog buoy, the Swordfish landed on the third attempt with visibility down to 50 yards. Patrols were carried out in all weather conditions and on September 22, Swordfish HS.381 B piloted by Sub Lt B.I. Barlowe and Sub Lt J.Boyd as observer took off with depth charges. A U-boat was detected on the surface and the ship informed. Swordfish LS.281 C took off piloted by Sub Lt P. T. Gifford with observer Lt J. H. G. Tapscott armed with rockets. Both Swordfish moved in and attacked independently but both missed due to the heavy return gunfire. It was obvious that a composite unit as used on the escort carriers would have been ideal but this was never employed on CAM-ships. The problem of the Swordfish vulnerability was to plague the crews until the end. On the convoy in question, six merchant ships were sunk, as were three escorts and one was damaged for the sinking of two U-boats. Three more MAC-ships came into service in October 1943 thus making eight operational by that time. On October 8 the *Rapana* was at sea with convoy SC.143 when a U-boat was reported shadowing astern. Taking off, the first Swordfish crashed but the others made several attacks on U-boats claiming one damaged. Two merchant ships were sunk on this convoy and two U-boats were destroyed. Although the escorts had sunk them, the odds were getting better.

By March 1944 some 18 MAC-ships were operational. Two, the *Gadila* and *Macoma* the latter commissioned later, were drawn from the Royal Netherlands Navy and No 860 Squadron was formed as a pool aircraft squadron for them. U-boat activities had declined as a result of MAC-ship and land based anti-submarine aircraft. Thus it was in March/April 1944 that MAC-ships ferried 212 aircraft in 11 voyages from New York to England for the invasion of Normandy. As many as four MAC-ships could be used in a convoy but the more usual ration was two. Even when a U-boat was sighted, however, things did not always work out. For example, M Flight of No 836 Squadron embarked in the *Empire Mackendrick* and G Flight embarked in

the *Ancylus* sailing from England on May 19, 1944 with convoy ON.237. On the afternoon of May 25 the convoy picked up U-boat signals and three Swordfish took off; M2 piloted by Sub Lt D. Shaw, observer Sub Lt H. W. M. Hodges, TAG Leading Airman J. M. King took off from *Empire Mackendrick*, G.1 piloted by Lt O. C. Johnstone, observer Sub Lt J. K. G. Taylor, TAG Leading Airman J. Buckland and G.2 piloted by Sub Lt B. J. Cooper, observer Sub Lt W. M. Owen, TAG Leading Airman F. J. Turner from *Ancylus*.

After sighting the U-boat the three Swordfish shadowed it for a time and then made a co-ordinated attack. All the rockets missed and heavy flak damaged all three Swordfish. A Swordfish of P Flight embarked in *Adula* went out after a U-boat but had engine failure and landed in the sea. The Swordfish unfortunately sank rather quickly taking the large dinghy, which had failed to inflate, and two of the individual crew members' dinghies. The three crew hung on to one small dinghy until they were rescued, unconscious, 50 minutes later by a schooner out from Nova Scotia. Another Swordfish crew from the *Empire Maccoll* piloted by Sub Lt W. G. Coates were sent out with another aircraft to cover a convoy which at that time was about 500 miles out from Ireland. Heavy fog came down and both aircraft asked permission to return. The first, being nearer, landed-on safely but by the time the other got back the ship was enshrouded in fog. It was told to head for land, at that time about 275 miles away and eventually force landed in Ireland without any damage. Expecting to be interned the crew were treated royally before they escaped by flying out with the help of the RAF to St. Angelo, and then to Maydown.

With the introduction of schnorkel equipment in U-boats it became even more difficult to detect them and one pilot fired all his rockets off at a big fish! Crews could hardly be blamed when weather was critical and fog and mist prevalent. Another problem that came up was that of whales. These great creatures would surface as a large brown shape with a vertical lump admidships and then dive again leaving a wake but no air bubbles. Three MAC-ships escorting convoy ON.240 once kept one Swordfish aloft all day until dusk checking whether wakes were whales or U-boats!

Flying routine convoy protection usually meant two MAC-ships working together as a unit. Search patrols were always at the side or ahead of convoys. An astern patrol could be disasterous for a slow Swordfish if the wind strengthened. On one occasion this happened and the ship watched until the Swordfish disappeared off the radar screen astern — never to be seen again. Each MAC-ship did a 12 hour turn of duty but if a U-boat sighting report came in all the aircraft would be launched from both. The small decks and poor weather were an inducement to accidents but these were few. Badly damaged Swordfish were usually stripped of all equipment and dumped over the side. Small amounts of damage or lack of spares usually resulted in the aircraft being lashed to the flight deck for the rest of the voyage. If a grain MAC-ship was with the convoy it wasn't so bad. With the small hangar they had more room for spares and on one occasion a Swordfish on *Miralda* chewed the tail of another while running up. A spare tailplane was transferred from the sister MAC-ship, *Empire Macalpine*, so keeping the aircraft serviceable.

Sightings and attacks continued to be made. In April 1945 a Swordfish of Y Flight in *Empire Macalpine* made several with depth charges. The depth charge was not normally used as it was not considered suitable for a surface attack, and herein lies a story. In 1944 all flights were instructed that prior to pre-convoy work-up off the Isle of Arran, all crews would drop two depth charges each on two sorties. This was somewhat alarming

because aircraft and crews had been lost when the smaller type of depth charge exploded as it hit the surface due to the failure of the hydro-static pistol. On one occasion Sub Lt B. J. Cooper of G Flight had watched the Flight's efforts and went in to drop the 11/12 depth charges. The last one went off on impact with the surface sending out a strong shock wave. This did an enormous amount of damage but the crew did not know how much. The air-craft went tail heavy and the dinghy sprang out (those on the ship thought it to be a body) but the engine still ran and when Cooper tried the controls they appeared to be alright except that with full backward trim both arms were needed to pull the stick back. Sub Lt Cooper eventually landed-on safely but his Swordfish was a write off. Several of the fuselage panels hung about, longerons and ribs were broken and the lower mainplane cross embers were, in some cases held together only by the blast plate for the rocket rails. Sub Lt Cooper was informed that he was the first pilot to survive one of the depth charges going off. Subsequently it became a standing order to fit special vanes to the depth charges which sheered off on impact. These vanes had in fact been stan-dard equipment for some time but for some reason had not been used.

The last contact between a Swordfish and U-boat was on April 20, 1945 when one from the *Empire Macandrew*, escorting con-voy ON.298, dropped two depth charges on a periscope, with no results. On May 21, 1945, the last operational squadron to fly the Swordfish, No 836, was disbanded. In its time it had been the largest squadron in the FAA with a flight of three or four Swordfish to each of the 19 MAC-ships. When the *Empire Mackay* arrived in England, the flight of her Swordfish from her deck was the last operational flight of Swordfish in the history of the Fleet Air Arm.

Top left: Just leaving another MAC-ship, this time the *Macalpine* in the winter of 1943. The short flight deck is most apparent in this picture./*J. T. Canham*

Centre left, above: Swordfish P2 over an Atlantic convoy. This aircraft was borrowed from *Macabe* after a disastrous period on *Macmahon* and subsequently was re-lettered./*J. T. Canham*

Centre left, below: Starting up Swordfish on open flight decks could be a trying experience, especially during winter months. Here one named Benarty has been coaxed into life on the deck of *Macalpine* early in 1944./*J. T. Canham*

Bottom left: Although this collapsed oleo of LS.316 on June 17, 1944 aboard *Macmahon* would be no trouble ashore it meant that this aircraft had to be stripped and ditched./*J. T. Canham*

Above: B2 of *Macmahon* comes in close after a patrol. These were usually flown ahead or down the sides of the convoy by individual aircraft./*J. T. Canham*

In retrospect, MAC-ships had made 170 round trips with Atlantic convoys, a total of 4 447 days at sea of which 3 057 were in convoy. Flying took place on 1 183 of these days during which 4 177 sorties were flown, 12 attacks made on U-boats none of which were sunk. It is however, true to say that since the in-troduction of the MAC-ships into the convoys that U-boats had little or no success against any convoy containing them.

69

Cartoon characters

Above: HS.275 J of No1 Naval Air Gunners School at Yarmouth, Canada has 'J Wellington Wimpy' a character from the Popeye cartoons. Other Swordfish were also adorned with them./*Public Archives of Canada*

Centre left: Not easily seen is an outline portrait of Donald Duck on this Swordfish NH.F NF.410 of No 119 Squadron, RAF just above the ASV radome./*IWM*

Bottom left: Not many Swordfish seemed to carry the type of adornment that was popular with the RAF but Dirty Dick I would appear to be the name of the pirate character on this Stringbag./*IWM*

Right: Swordfish LS.434 B3 'Benvorlich' of No 836 Squadron aboard MAC-Ship *Macalpine* in 1944. The baker's head was in black and white on a grey background with the aircraft flight number eg. B1, B2 on the headband. The number on the fuselage was also in black. Note the bent propeller tip./*J. T. Canham*

Flying Dutchman

Above: A line up of four Swordfish of No 860 Squadron, Royal Netherlands Navy, at Maydown in Northern Ireland./*R Neth Navy*

Centre left: A Dutch Swordfish off No 860 Squadron catches the first wire as it lands aboard MAC-ship *Gadila*. Note the narrowness of the flight deck./*R. Neth Navy*

Bottom left: Swordfish NE.951 S1 of No 860 Squadron immediately after landing aboard *Gadila*. Note the Dutch orange triangle on the top of the rudder./*R. Neth Navy*

Top right: One of the Dutch Swordfish of No 860 Squadron comes to grief./*R. Neth Navy*

Centre right: As one Dutch Swordfish with wings folded taxies forward, the deck party gets ready to receive another coming up astern./*R. Neth Navy*

Bottom right: Swordfish S3 with its tail already up starts its take off run from *Gadila* armed with rockets and bombs.

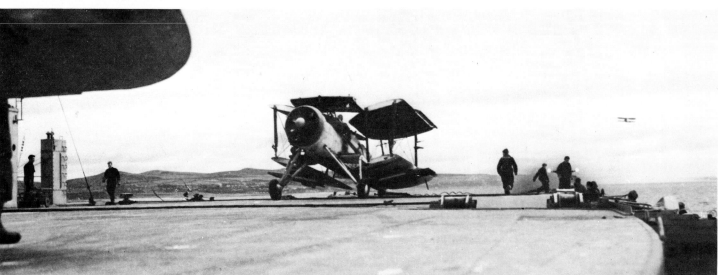

Canadian capers

In 1942 the British Admiralty initiated the formation of a naval air gunners' school in Canada under the British Commonwealth Air Training Plan. Apart from satisfying the need to have such an establishment in a country other than the embattled United Kingdom, it also provided a supply of newly trained TAGs for the squadrons forming up in America with Lend-Lease aircraft.

Thus, on January 1, 1943, No 1 Naval Air Gunners' School RCAF, was formed at Yarmouth, Novia Scotia to train TAGs. Initially Swordfish HS.209, 260, 261, 263, 264, 265, 266, 268 and 275 were on strength with five more added in February, and 12 more in March. At its peak the unit had 67 Swordfish on strength. Other Swordfish arrived in dribs and drabs until 105 had arrived in Canada, 99 Mk II and six Mk IIIs. Most were in standard wartime camouflage. Later, some Mk IIs were converted into Mk IVs by fitting a coupe top under Modification Order 408, this work being carried out in 1944. Eight were later modified as target drogue towers and apart from the camouflage topsides, the undersides sported yellow and black stripes. These Swordfish, all modified from the Mk IV were hybrid aircraft and no mark number was ever allotted to them. A few Swordfish were also used by No 6 Bombing and Gunnery School and a number of smaller units. Some were not used at all and were probably cannibalised to keep the other Swordfish flying.

After the war the Swordfish were all taken over by the War Assets Corporation and stored in the hangars at the former RCAF base at Mount Hope, Ontario, pending disposal. In September 1945, HMS *Seaborn*, the Royal Navy's flying establishment at Dartmouth asked permission to dispose of 22 Swordfish and three Walrus aircraft. Obviously it was intended to destroy them but the RCN saw a use for them and quickly arranged a stay of execution with the British Admiralty while storage space at Eastern Passage was found. In October after a series of conferences between the higher echelons of the RCAF and RCN an agreement was signed giving the RCAF management of all RCN shore-based air activities and this included air stores, supporting services, major aircraft repairs and maintenance. Commander H. J. Gibbs, RCNVR, the commanding officer of the Air Section at Eastern Passage took over on November 21, 1945, with three officers, six ratings and six civilians. The first job was the mustering of stores from the British for the newly aquired aircraft. One Swordfish was test inspected to provide the section with a cross country communications aircraft. Everyone pitched in to help renovate the buildings and get everywhere ship shape. The Swordfish were then formed into No 743 Fleet Requirements Unit and were for general purposes only. The new career of these veteran aircraft was, however, shortlived.

In 1946 with the formation of the RCN air arm reserve an immediate demand arose for flying instruction aircraft and as it was proposed to use Harvards, the Swordfish was relegated to ground instruction airframes. It was however, decided to provide as many reserve units as possible with a Swordfish so that personnel received practical instruction. Some of the Swordfish were tuned

up and ferried to their destinations among the 11 Naval Divisions across the country by air. Many of the flights were far from routine. The following is an example.

Three Swordfish took off on September 17, 1946, bound for HMCS *Unicorn* at Saskatoon, HMCS *Tecumseh* at Calgary and HMCS *Nonsuch* at Edmonton. The first stop was at Megantic, Quebec, followed by Montreal, Trenton, Toronto, North Bay, Kapuskasing, Armstrong, Kenora and Winnipeg. Leaving the latter one of the pilots discovered he had a broken fuel line and had to land in a farmer's field. One of the other Swordfish returned to Winnipeg with the damaged fuel line, got it repaired and flew back. The journey continued through Neepawa, Yorkton and Saskatoon, where one Swordfish remained. They then went on to Medicine Hat and Calgary where the two aircraft caused some excitement by landing on the parade ground. The last one set off for Edmonton where the pilot caused even more excitement by landing in Edmonton Ball Park. It had completed 2 400 miles in 10 days after some 39 hours 35 minutes flying time.

These ground training Swordfish continued to give sterling training service until they were all finally scrapped.

Far left: A Swordfish II (IV) HS. 487 F3 of No1 Air Gunnery School after a crash at Lawrencetown on October 17, 1944. White paint has been hastily applied over wartime camouflage./*Public Archives of Canada*

Top: One of the few Swordfish IIIs to go to Canada was this magnificent specimen NR.994 seen here at RCNAS Dartmouth. It was not delivered until March 1946, and thus did not have the canopy modification. /*Public Archives of Canada*

Above left: Getting in close for some formation practice is this unknown Swordfish II (IV) from No1 NAGS in 1944./*Public Archives of Canada*

Above right: Previous identity unknown. NS122 TH.M the preserved Swordfish held in the Canadian National Collection. /*Canadian Armed Forces*

Coastal Stringbags

One of the first and last operational formations to have the Swordfish operating under its wing was Coastal Command of the RAF. Before the war a number of Swordfish had come under this command at Gosport but the pioneer squadron was No 812 which at various times operated from North Coates, Thorney Island, Detling and St Eval. From May 1940 to March 1941, Swordfish from 812 operated with auxiliary fuel tanks in the rear cockpit and had a crew of two. Targets were usually oil tanks at Calais or invasion barges at Rotterdam. Previous to this 825 Squadron had briefly come under Coastal Command when from May 1940 to July it operated from Detling. During May it operated in support of the British retreat from Dunkirk. Operating in daylight its aircraft attacked tanks, vehicles and enemy troops, suffering heavy losses in the process. The CO at this time — significantly — was Lt Cdr E. Esmonde. In July aircraft of No 825 attacked barges near Rotterdam and layed mines in the Scheldt estuary. Other FAA squadrons shore based under Coastal Command were Nos 811, 819 and No 119 Squadron of the RAF. The latter was formed from a flight of No 415 (RCAF) Squadron which in July 1944 was operating Wellingtons and Albacores. When 415 converted to the Halifax, the Albacore flight was retained by Coastal Command and formed into the new squadron under Sqd Ldr J. I. J. Davies, DFC. It came under

No 155 G.R. Wing at RAF Manston but operated from Bircham Newton while in the UK or airfield B.83 in Belgium. It became obvious after a time that the Albacore would have to be replaced and oddly enough it fell to the aircraft it was designed to replace to take over its role. The first two Swordfish made available for training appeared in January 1945 and by the end of the month 10 were ready for operations.

The first operational patrol was carried out on February 6, 1945 by Fg Off Rabbets. Thereafter the Swordfish were used on day and night patrols over the Channel looking for E-boats and midget submarines (known as 'bipers' No 119 Squadron). By the end of March four midget submarines had been sunk, three E-boats damaged and probable damage to other craft. On April 12 while on patrol Plt Off Goundry in Swordfish F caught two midget submarines on the surface and blew one completely out of the water. In May the squadron were informed that they were to move to Copenhagen but this fell through. Back in February the squadron had received a new CO Sqd Ldr N. Williamson who on May 4 took off with his navigator Fl Lt D. G. Matkin in Swordfish P on a patrol. At 1430 they found a midget submarine, which appeared to be stranded on a sand bank. Realising his depth charges were useless for this attack, Sqd Ldr Williamson flew back to B.83 and re-armed with bombs. He attacked the submarine with the bombs and oil quickly spread on the sea. There was no sign of the crew. This was the celebrated midget submarine which was attacked only 3½ hours before the German surrender. An anti-E-boat patrol was flown on May 11 but the war in Europe was over and on May 22, 1945, 14 Swordfish (plus one that later went u/s) flew back across the Channel in formation to land at Bircham Newton. No 119 Squadron was renumbered to become No 1 Movement Training Unit but with the final end of the war this too was disbanded.

Bottom left: This photo shows surviving members of No 825 Squadron in 1940 after the harrowing time attacking targets in support of the retreating British Expeditionary Force near Dunkirk and Calais./*via J. K. Cannon*

Top right: The all black Swordfish of No 119 Squadron, RAF, dispersed at Bircham Newton. They operated from a sea of mud in Belgium called Knocke-le-Zoute airfield./*IWM*

Centre right: NF343 N.H.O was one of the all black Swordfish. Numbers and codes were in red./*Ministry of Defence*

Below: A pilot approaches Swordfish 3A of No 812 Squadron at RAF North Coates in November 1940. At this time 812 were operating under Coastal Command and striking at targets across the Channel./*Fox Photos*

In mufti

Canada/USA

Although the vast majority of Canadian Swordfish from Yarmouth went to the RCN, some were scrapped and seven others were sold off to a Mr Simmons of Courtland for £15 each. Simmonds was a genuine eccentric with a passion for collecting mechanical items. At his death it was discovered he had accumulated 169 motor cars dating from 1928; 107 motor-cycles from 1917; 40 odd tractors and steam engines; 32 Yale training aircraft; 26 stationary petrol engines; 15 Bren carriers and seven Swordfish. He also had tons of spares including 34 Cheetah engines for Anson aircraft, as well as 57 assorted guns to keep people away from his collection. These were used fairly frequently and in 1968 when a troupe of travelling motor-cycle acrobats tried to commandeer some of his motor-cycle collection they were shot first and arrested afterwards. Once an attacker that broke in shot him seven times but he survived only to die not long after from pneumonia. An auction of his collection was arranged and this aroused considerable interest in Canada and elsewhere. Bidding was by number only and 4 000 would-be buyers registered to bid while some 50 000 people turned up as spectators. The seven Swordfish had suffered over the years, having been left in the open, but Simmons had run the engines up at various times.

Top left: The nose of HS256 showing that when this photo was taken it was already being used for spares to keep ZS.BNU flying./*D. Becker*

Left: The fuselage of one of two Swordfish bought by Englishman Nick Pocock from the sale at Simmons farm in Canada./*N. Pocock*

Top right: This poor, but rare photo shows ZS.BNU ex- HS.255 still in wartime camouflage in a hangar at Benoni in South Africa after the war./*D. Becker*

Centre right: Swordfish LS.326 disguised as G.AJVH during the time it was used by Fairey for communications and display work. The colours were blue and silver and this was taken at White Waltham in May 1956. /*A. J. Jackson*

Above right: The same aircraft, LS.326/G.AJVH taken at White Waltham in May 1964 after it had been restored to its military markings./*A. J. Jackson*

All were standing on their undercarriage with the wings removed and stored nearby. Several had yellow and black stripes and two had the rear cockpit removed as though for drogue towing although there was no towing equipment to suggest this. All fabric had long since gone and advanced deterioration had set in on all the Swordfish. Two had lost their Pegasus engines but these were found nearby while the others, despite being run up regularly had long since lost their compression. Most of the Swordfish were capable of restoration to some degree but decay and the general lack of spares meant static displays. (It is interesting to note at this stage that the National Air Museum at Ottawa had approached Simmons in 1965 about one of the Swordfish and he eventually sold them one. It was so corroded that it was not possible to trace its identity and after restoration by the RCN and The Fairey Aviation Co Ltd of Canada it was allotted the serial number NS.122, an aircraft struck off strength in Novemebr 1945). The Swordfish were sold on the last day of the sale and despite rumours to the contrary, prices were in the £300 - £550 range. Two were purchased by a manufacturer of mobile caravans who hoped to restore them to flying condition. An Air Cadet squadron bought one for static show and a group of men from western Ontario also hoped to fly the one they bought. The best of the bunch was bought by the National Air Museum on behalf of the Fleet Air Arm Museum at Yeovilton. This was flown to the UK in an RAF Belfast transport with the fuselage and wings going to the RAF Museum at Hendon and the engine to the FAA Museum. The last two were purchased by Nick Pocock, an Englishman living in Texas. Mr Pocock, an experienced pilot, planned to sell one Swordfish to fund restoration of the other to flying condition. Asking price for the spare aircraft as this book went to press was 6 000 dollars.

South Africa

In August 1948 a South African newspaper mentioned the sale of two Fairey Swordfish with engines and spares at RNAS Wingfield, Capetown. These were in fact purchased by Eddie McConnell with the idea of using them for banner towing. They were registered ZS. BNU and BNV, their previous identities being HS.255 and 256 respectively. In fact only ZS.BNU was converted for use and was based at Benoni aerodrome most of its time. What little flying it did ended in 1952 in a hangar fire. ZS.BNV remained in the Owenair hangar at Youngfield still in RN camouflage and minus its propeller until at least 1957. By early 1958 it had been, by accident or otherwise, burnt out and for a short time its remains were dumped behind the hangar.

United Kingdom

Immediately after the war there were many military aircraft put up for disposal and one can be forgiven for seeing little use for ex-FAA Swordfish. However, one was sold to E. Percival the aircraft manufacturer but for what purpose he does not recall. Six were sold via Fairey to Pest Control Ltd (now Fisons) of Cambridge. They planned to convert them with spray bars for use in the Sudan. The plan fell through but the Swordfish, minus all fabric, were in a field next to the factory before being sold for scrap. One however was retained by Fairey who wanted it as a musum piece. LS.326 was the serial but Sir Richard Fairey had the aircraft made airworthy and it was flown by company test pilots at various aeronautical functions. To continue flying it had to be registered G.AJVH and in this form was to be seen at air shows and was used as a communications aircraft before reverting to its military marking for a film, after which it went to the FAA Museum.

Grand old Lady

The last and only airworthy Swordfish in the world today is LS.326, the one Fairey originally saved to be a museum piece. It has pride of place with the FAA Historic Flight at RNAS Yeovilton and is in big demand for air displays.

LS.326 was built at the Blackburn Sherburn-in-Elmet factory in 1943 but there is little record of its wartime service except for communications and training work. It was hangared at Heston but in October 1947, back in Service markings it was flown by Peter Twiss, the Fairey chief test pilot, to Hamble for refurbishing. A year later it was transferred to White Waltham for storage. In September 1954 it was again taken to Hamble for restoration work. During 1955 a tremendous amount of work and time was spent in finding the necessary parts and getting it recovered with fabric. In October, Geoffrey Alington made a test flight at an all up weight of 7 000lb and achieved 127 knots. LS.326 then became G.AJVH for a short time in the well known Fairey blue and silver markings of its civil fleet. Then 20th Century Fox asked if they could use it in the film, *Sink The Bismack*. So in 1959 LS.326 went back into Service markings to represent the leader's aircraft of the first wave of Swordfish that attacked *Bismack*. The colour scheme is the one carried to this day. The following year, 1960, all the aircraft side of Fairey was taken over by Westland Aircraft and in September of that year LS.326 was handed over to RNAS Yeovilton. So, after 15 years adrift the Swordfish returned to the FAA. The Board of Admiralty said that the aircraft could be kept flying so long as its condition remained good after which it must revert to static display. By March 1965 the spares problem was becoming critical and flying time was running out on the engine. Widespread appeals were made but the answer was found nearer home. The Imperial War Museum held a Swordfish and eventually the FAA exchanged the engine in their aircraft for one in good condition but not airworthy. Over 550 man hours were put in to renovate the engine and on January 17, 1970 the Pegasus burst into life at the first crank. This engine it is hoped will allow LS.326 to continue flying at least into the 1980s, when it will surely be the last of the Swordfish.

Below: NF.389 in its Service colours prior to being used in the film *Sink The Bismarck.* It now resides at RNAS Lee-on-Solent where it is turned out for open days or the Taranto re-union when it graces the front of the officers' mess. Other surviving Swordfish are NF.370 held in the Imperial War Museum and HS.618 displayed in the Fleet Air Arm Museum at Yeovilton. The latter is painted to depict the aircraft that Esmonde flew on his tragic last flight./*A. J. Jackson*

Bottom: What better way to end this book than with a superb picture of the world's last flying Swordfish, LS.326./*Rolls Royce*